Poems of Richard Barnfield

Poems of Richard Barnfield

Edited by George Klawitter

iUniverse, Inc.
New York Lincoln Shanghai

Poems of Richard Barnfield

iUniverse books may be ordered through booksellers or by contacting:

iUniverse
2021 Pine Lake Road, Suite 100
Lincoln, NE 68512
www.iuniverse.com
1-800-Authors (1-800-288-4677)

ISBN-13: 978-0-595-36798-6 (pbk)
ISBN-13: 978-0-595-67420-6 (cloth)
ISBN-13: 978-0-595-81213-4 (ebk)
ISBN-10: 0-595-36798-4 (pbk)
ISBN-10: 0-595-67420-8 (cloth)
ISBN-10: 0-595-81213-9 (ebk)

Printed in the United States of America

Contents

Richard Barnfield

We know few facts about Richard Barnfield. He was born in 1574 at Norbury, Staffordshire, but we do not know when he died or where he is buried. He attended Brasenose College at Oxford, matriculating in 1589 at the age of fifteen, and earned his B.A. in 1592. His publishing career began in 1594 and ended eleven years later. After the second edition of his fifth book in 1605, Richard Barnfield appears only once in public documents: he is mentioned in a 1616 inquisition for Sir Richard Lee. In that year, Barnfield was living in Shropshire. At the age of forty-three, he slips out of history. Some of the data we thought we had on him has proved to be incorrect. The will and inventory attributed to Barnfield and first printed by Alexander B. Grosart in 1876 have been proved by Andrew Worrell to be the will and inventory of Barnfield's father. In his research, Worrell has also discovered that Barnfield was disinherited by his father in favor of Barnfield's younger brother.

We can, of course, learn much about Barnfield from his poetry. We can surmise from the early shepherd poems that he was pleasant and light-hearted. Later poetry becomes more somber as the poet tackles the topics of patronage and conscience. His is a talented pen, and if he is not ranked with Marlowe and Shakespeare, he is certainly better than many of the other minor Elizabethan poets as anyone who reads his verse discovers. We need to keep Barnfield in print because he has been a neglected voice in the Renaissance, the first English poet openly to write pastoral of one man's love for another man.

I include in this edition all of the works attributed to Barnfield (by virtue of his having acknowledged his authorship in print) and two early works which he may have disclaimed in his preface to *Cynthia* but which were probably his: *Greenes Funeralls* has been attributed to him for almost a century, and *Orpheus His Journey to Hell* has received much critical attention in recent years, most of it inclined to favor Barnfield authorship.

The "dubia" poems remain a problem. Two are most certainly by Barnfield: the lines addressed to Sir John Spenser (because Barnfield's name follows them in the Isham manuscript), and "The Unknowne Sheepheards Complaint" (because it is attributed to him in *Englands Helicon*). The manuscript in which the former poem is found may very well be a miscellany assembled by anyone. Just because Barnfield's name is attached to one poem does not mean he authored all the pieces. Indeed, the John Spenser poem is the only Isham manuscript poem that sounds like something Barnfield would write: its poetic resonance is unmistakably Barnfield's. But all the "dubia" are included here so that an editorial error, if any, be inclusive rather than exclusive.

Orpheus His Journey to Hell has been checked against the British Library copy. *The Affectionate Shepheard* has been checked against the copy held by the Folger Shakespeare Library, and *Cynthia* against the copy held by the Huntington Library. Punctuation has been retained as found in the first editions. I have left stand copious commas in the text where today we would avoid them. Barnfield (or his printer) seems to have intended them as breath marks, e.g., in *The Complaint of Poetrie*. Indentations of lines usually result from printers' decisions, and I have omitted indentations except where spacing lends grace. I have silently emended "i" to "j" as well as "u" to "v" where necessary.

The 1990 edition of Barnfield's poetry included an extensive introduction and copious end notes, but this present edition has neither extended introduction nor end notes because the verses read quite well on their own. Barnfield's lines are not obscure. Readers who wish to pursue various references can consult the 1990 edition, which unfortunately is no longer readily available. I hope the present edition keeps his poetry close to both established and new scholars of the English Renaissance.

George Klawitter
St. Edward's University

Greenes Funeralls

By R B. Gent.

Printed at London by John Danter, and are
To be sold at his House in Hosier-Lane nere
Holbourne-Conduit.
1594.

To the Gentlemen Readers Health.

Gentle Reader, I once readd of a King, that divided the day into three parts; the First hee spent in Prayer, the Second in hearing of his Subjects causes, and the last in delight and pleasure of his body: So (Gentle Reader) I hope thou wilt spend one daies pleasure in reading this Pamphlet, wherin no curious theame is writt uppon; but certaine Poemes, Entituled: *Greenes Funeralls*. Which contrarie to the Authours expectation I have nowe published, for it was his private study at idle times. Gentlemen, fine wits are quicknde with one cup of pure wine, where many woulde make them dull; And this small Pamphlet may recreate your mindes, when large Volumes would but cloy and weary you: Now if the Authors paines, and the Printers labour may be acceptable to thee (Gentle Reader) the one hath his hyer, and the other his desire.

Yours in all curtesie, John Danter.

SONNET I

Why should my Pen presume to write his praise,
And hee in perfect mould of *Vertue* framde?
Why should my Muse sing of his happie daies,
And he the marke, at which Dame *Nature* aimed?
    Why rather should I not such vertues show,
    That such pure golde from drosse each man may know?
But cease my Muse, why dost thou take in hand so great a Taske:
Which to perform a greater wit, than *Mercuries* would aske?
For judgement *Jove*, for Learning deepe, he still *Apollo* seemde:
For floent Tongue, for eloquence, men *Mercury* him deemde.
For curtesie suppose him *Guy*, or *Guyons* somewhat lesse:

His life and manners though I would, I cannot halfe expresse.
Nor *Mouth*, nor *Minde*, nor *Muse* can halfe declare,
His *Life*, his *Love*, his *Laude*, so excellent they were.

SONNET II

Fortune, hates not, them that hate her:
Fortune, loves not, them that love her:
Fortune, would, and cannot rate her:
Fortune, shall, and must remove her.
    And though fickle *Fortune* smile:
    It is but for a little while.

Greene lovde *Fortune* foolish Man,
Foolish man, why lovde he so?
And her foolish race he ran,
Foolish race thats run with woe.
    Woe than (Alas) was lesse misused?
    Now (Alas) is more abused?

But let *Fowles* and foolish fellowes,
Barke and byte their belly fill:
It is not spightfull Envies bellowes,
That can kindie fire still.
    No booke pleases all that come:
    None so bad but pleases some.

SONNET III

Yee dainty *Damsels* of *Dianes* Traine,
That long to dally, with your loved *Lords*:
And you brave Gallant, high resolved *Lords*.
That love to gaze, upon your stately *Starrs*.

He he is dead, that kild you with disdaine:
And often fedde your friendly hopes againe.

He he is dead, that wrote of your delights:
That wrote of *Ladies*, and of *Parramours*:
Of budding beautie, and hir branched leaves,
Of sweet content in royall Nuptialls,
    He he is dead, that kild you with disdaine:
    And often fed your friendly hopes againe.

His gadding Muse, although it ran of love,
Yet did hee sweetly morralize, his songs:
Ne ever gave the looser cause to laugh,
Ne men of Judgment, for to be offended.
    But as he often kild them with disdaine:
    So did he often feede their hopes againe.

And though he often told of things to come.
In love more like a Prophet than a Poet:
Yet did he wisely interlace the one,
With *Sages* sayings, ever mixt among.
    And though he often fedde their pleasing paine:
    Yet did he often kill them with disdaine.

Wherefore yee dainty *Damsels* of renowne,
That long to dallie, with your loved *Lords*:
And you brave Gallant, worthy noble *Lords*,
That love to dandle in your *Ladies* lapps.
    Come hither come, and lend your mouths to Fame:
    That meanes to sound, his never dying name.

SONNET IIII

Come from the Muses well *Minerva*,
Come and bring a Coronet:

To crowne his head, that doth deserve,
A greater gift than *Colinet*.

Come from *Bacchus* bowre *Silenus*,
Come and bring some good-ale grout:
For to sprinckle *Vino-plenus*:
All his foolish face about.

Come thou hither sweet *Amyntas*
All on a silver sounding Swanne:
Come and teach this fond *A-mint-Asse*,
Leave the game as hee began.

Come thou hither my friend so pretty,
All riding on a Hobby-Horse:
Either make thy selfe more witty:
Or againe renew thy force:

Come and decke his browes with baies,
That deserves immortall praise.

SONNET V

Amend thy stile who can: who can amend thy stile?
    For sweet conceit.
    Alas the while,
That ever any such, as thou shouldst die,
    By fortunes guile,
    Amids thy meate.
Pardon (Oh pardon) me that cannot shew,
    My zealous love.
    Yet shalt thou prove,
That I will ever write in thy behove:
    Gainst any dare,
    With thee compare.

It is not *Hodge-poke* nor his fellow deare,
  That I doe feare:
  As shall appeare.
But him alone that is the Muses owne,
  And eke my friend,
  Whome to the end,
My muse must ever honor and adore:
  Doe what I can.
  To praise the man,
It is impossible for me that am,
  So far behinde.
  Yet is my minde,
As forward as the best, if wit so would
  With will agree.
  But since I see,
  It will not bee:
I am content, my folly to confesse:
  And pardon crave.
  Which if I have,
My Fortunes greater than my former fall:
  I must confesse.

But if he other wise esteeme of me,
Than as a friend or one that honors thee:
Then is my labor lost, my care consumde.
Because I hate the hope, that so presumde.

SONNET VI

Of *Tel-tales* tell my muse,
  Of such as love to lie:
Of such as use, for to abuse,
  Their friends and no cause why.

Of such and none but such,
>My pen shall write his pleasure:
And them at large I meane to tuch,
>When I have time and leasure.
My rime is rude, what then?
>Yet will it serve the turne:
To notifie such wicked men,
>As doe deserve to burne.
As doe deserve to burne said I?
>Nay worse: that ought to feele,
The raging force and crueltie:
>Of old *Ixions* wheele.
But least I should this mourning Muse retaine:
Ile fall into an other kinde of vaine.

SONNET VII

Though perchance it seeme to some but a toy and a trifle,
Seeme to some in vaine, to bestowe but a part of an houre,
In penning Poemes: in hon'ring him with a Poeme.
Yet I appeale to the pen of pierelesse Poet *Amyntas*,
Matchles *Amintas* minde, to the minde of Matchles *Amintas*,
Sweete bonny *Phillis* love, to the love of sweet bonny *Phillis*,
Whether pen, or minde, or love, of *Phillis Amintas*
Love, or minde, or pen, of pen-love-minder *Amintas*:
Thinke of him (perhaps) as some doe thinke of *Amintas*:
Oh that I might be lovde, of *Phillis* lover: *Amintas*.
Oh that I might be thought, as I thinke of *Phillis*: *Amintas*.
Oh that I might be judgde as I judge of *Phillis*: *Amintas*:
Then would I never care for such base beggarly make-bookes
That in veigh against the dead, like deadly maligners.
What if he were a man, as bad or worse than a Hel-hound?
As shall I thinke that he was as bad or worse than a Hel-hound?

Yet it ill became sweete mindes to haunt in *Avernus*:

Ill became such Cutes, to barke at a poore silly carcas

Some had cause to mone, and mourne, & murmur against him:

Others none at all, yet none at all, so against him.

For my selfe I wish, that none had written against him

But such men which had just cause t'have written against him.

SONNET VIII

Muse give place to my mone, and mone give place to my musing:

One for an others cause, and one for cause of an other.

First to behold him dead: last to behold him alive.

And thou Shepheards Swaine, that keepes thy sheepe by the mountaines,

(Mountaines) of *Sicily*, and sweet *Arcadian* Iland,

Oh *Meliboeus*: leave, Oh leave any more to be mourning.

For though his Art bee dead, yet shall it ever abide:

Ever abide, to the end: light, as a light to the rest.

Rest that have wrot of love: and the delights of a lover.

But by the sweete consent, of *Pan* and *Marsias* ofspringe.

Sweet consent of a *Saint* so sweet, of a *Fowle* and a foule one

Greenes but a foolish man: and such as him doe defend.

Yet will I ever write both to defend and offend:

For to defend his friends, and to offend his foes.

SONNET IX

Greene, is the pleasing Object of an eie:

Greene, pleasde the eies of all that lookt uppon him.

Greene, is the ground of everie Painters die:

Greene, gave the ground, to all that wrote upon him.

Nay more the men, that so Eclipst his fame:
Purloynde his Plumes, can they deny the same?

Ah could my Muse, old Maltaes Poet passe,
(If any Muse could passe, old Maltaes Poet)
Then should his name be set in shining brasse,
In shining brasse for all the world to show it.
That little children, not as yet begotten
Might royallize his fame when he is rotten.

But since my Muse begins to vaile hir wings,
And flutter low upon the lowly Earth:
As one that sugred Sonnets, seldome singes,
Except the sound of sadnes, more than mirth,
To tell the worth of such a worthy man:
Ile leave it unto those, that better can.

Now may thy soule againe, goe take his rest
(His pleasant rest) in those eternall joyes
Where burning Tapers, still attend the blest
To light, and lighten them from all annoyes.
Goe then poore Poet, live and never die:
Ever, yet never but in miserie.

And as I came into the world unknowne,
Movde with compassion, of thy piteous plaint:
So will I now againe, my selfe go mone,
That durst presume, thy praise in verse to paint.
And if the Muses pardon, mine so weake:
I passe not of a pin, what others speake.

SONNET X

A Catalogue of certaine of his Bookes.

Camilla for the first and second part.
The *Card of Fancie*, and his *Tullies love*.
His *Nunquam Sera*, and his *Nightingale*.
His *Spanish Masquerado*, and his *Change*.
His *Menaphon*, and *Metamorphosis*.
His *Orpharion*, and the *Denmarke King*.
His *Censure*, and his *Loves Tritameron*.
His *Disputation*, and the *Death of him*,
That makes all *England* shed so many teares:
And many more that I have never seene
May witnes well unto the world his wit,
Had he so well, as well applied it.

SONNET XI

When my loathed life, had lost the light of *Olimpus*,
And descended downe, to the cursed caves of *Avernus*,
Never more had I thought, of men to be inlie molested,
    But now alas, I see my hope is vaine:
    My pleasure turned, to eternal paine.
For such foolish men, as I had never abused:
Never abused alas, yet alas, had ever abused:
Ever abused so, because so never abused.
    Not onely seeke to quench my kindled glorie,
    But also for to marre my *vertues* storie.
And though my life were lewd, Oh how it grieves me to thinke it.
Lewd as a life might be, from all good counsell abandond:
And given over up, to the out cast sense of a sinner.
    Yet might my end, have movd them to remorce:
    And not to reake their teene, on sillie corse.

SONNET XII

Father of *Heaven*, for thy mercies meekenes,
And thy sweete Sonnes sake, *Christ* the redeemer,
Pardon, Oh pardon, sinfull offender,
    Lord I beseech him.

And though his age, here on earth were a loathsome
Puddle of filthynes, inly poluted,
With all abuse, that can be devised,
    Yet was his ending;

Ending a myrrour, of a man molested,
One over-whelmed with his iniquities,
And to be holpen alone by the *Jesus*
    Saviour of all men.

ORPHEUS

His Journey to Hell
1595

To his Worshipfull good Friend,
M. Anthonie Copley, Esquier.

Good Sir, the Authour of this Poem, doubting at his first entrance, to entreat the acceptance of these his rude lines by any friend by name, hath instantlie sollicited mee (at whose request he doth publish the same in print) to dispose the dedication hereof to my best content: Wherfore, I have presumed to make you my choice, being the man that my best friendes and my selfe are greatly beholding unto for many respective favours: I (therfore,) humblie intreat you, that you will accept my good will, & pardon my boldnes: And withall (if in perusing it) you find any thing not fitting your judgment, your milde censure would friendlie overpasse it, considering that, *Nemo nascitur Artifex*: Wherin you shall so animate his yet unhartned Muse, as that at his next vacant houres, hee may better furnish some fitter Subjet. Which (if such happen into my handes) I will gladlie make you partaker of, to requite your favorable entertainment of these his unpolished labors: And bind me,

Yours in all dutie.
Thomas Johnes.

TO THE GENTLEMEN READERS

Heere have ye (Gentlemen) a Musick-man,
(The Infant muse of an imboldened pen:
Now if yee please t'adventure for a woman,
Descend yee down a while to Plutoes *den*
  Nor feare yee any Bugges whilst Orpheus *is there,*
  But rather to his musicke lend your listening eare.

15

Imperious Musicke, harmonie of Love,
Leads Orpheus *like a God through* Acharon*:*
Hels drierie shades and shapes it doeth remove,
And fair enchaunteth Pluto *to submission.*
     It frees the bonnie Bride Euridice *from hell,*
     So farre sweet Musicke was of force: and all was well.

But once when with a retrograde aspect,
Orpheus *reflected on the helles hee past:*
Then all his Musicke-gaine slipt to defect,
And all his Love with woe was overcast.
     & A president to Lovers in their Loves pursuit,
     Not to regard or grudge the paine that longs unto it.

Yet Orpheus *nerthelesse returnes from hell,*
From out the ruines of his fatall love:
Through Musickes mightie and alhallowed spell,
To shew that Musicke can all hels remoove,
     From out the mind, though neere so maine and manifold.
     Now read it (Gentlemen) if you please, my tale is told.

ORPHEUS HIS JOURNEY TO HELL

When as the world in her first golden time,
Frutefull in everie blessing did abound:
When *Floras* pride was alwaies in her prime,
And Winters wrath did ner' offend the ground
But without labour every thing encreased,
And pleasant sommers seasons never ceased.

No harsh aspect of heavens restlesse frame
Did alter earthly creatures in their kinde:
Each savage beast and bird that time was tame,
And all the world accorded in one minde.   10

For then dissention was a thing unknowne,
And seedes of envie and debate not sowne.

When as olde *Saturne* had in peace disposed,
His scepter and his glorious throne in heaven:
And in their severall kingdome had inclosed,
Each of his children and by portions even,
Making all several kings in severall places,
Devided to them all his giftes and graces.

Then did great *Jove* in peace succeede his Sire,
And *Neptune* bridled in the lawless seas;　　　　　　20
Pluto in hell amidst a world of fire,
Keeping tormented soules from rest and ease,
Orerules the hagges that in those dangerous moyles,
And to the Ghosts imposes endlesse toyles.

In this contented time was *Orpheus* borne,
Compos'd of purer mettell than a man:
Made mortall by the Gods in Natures scorne,
That earth might witnes how the heavens can
Inclose in Elementall shapes celestiall things,
Whose life from quintescence of heaven springs.　　　30

This pure composed shape the Gods endued
With their owne vertues, els had it been shame,
That he whose bodie from the heavens issued,
Should have a soule forg'd in a baser frame.
Thus did the Gods agree for to combine
A heavenly body and a soule divine.

This was that *Orpheus*, whose delightfull stringes,
Drew to their silver sound the sencelesse trees:
That still'd the musicke of the bubbling springs,
And staide the streames to heare his harmonies:　　　40

That made the savage beasts forsake their praie,
And gently come to heare sweet *Orpheus* play.

The craggie rockes that walles the Oceans bound,
Where *Neptune* keeps his watrie regiment,
Rose from their flinty roots to heare him sound,
And whil'st he sang, seem'd for to stand content.
The fishes left the seas to live ashore,
Which never heard of Musicks name before.

Thus liv'd he long the woonder of his time, `
Whose heaven-borne musicke wonne the love of all   50
Aspiring honor taught his fame to clime,
And made him live secure from thought of fall.
Till Fortune that orerules the state of kinges,
Did oreturne him, as she doth other things.

The pleasing poyson of self-killing Love,
At last made entrance to his mayden-heart:
Where once being anchored, never would remove,
But with sweet tickling wounds there bred his smart.
Yet did his wish prevaile his hope's effected,
His Love found love, and never was rejected.   60

But as it is in things being soonest growne,
Whose flowered blossoms every blast decayes:
And never stayes the Autumne to be mowne,
But floorishes and falles within few dayes:
So is't in love, which being quicklie sproong,
Dies oftentimes when as it is but yoong.

Euridice, the flower of flowering *Thrace*,
Whom *Orpheus* often in his ditties praised,
She that had all perfection in her face,
And at her face made every thing amazed: 70

For love of her *Orpheus* incurr'd this paine,
Though she with love requited love againe.

Being thus agreed in love, and both contented,
The day was pointed for their marriage right:
When most assur'd they soonest were prevented,
And sundred by unconstant Fortunes spight.
So by the meanes of a malignant power,
Their joyes began and ended in an hower.

The marriage day being come, and all things fit,
And *Hymeneus* rites now done and ended:　　　　　　　80
Home they returne, and at their banquets sit
With pleasures such, as to such meetings tended.
And when at home was ended all their sport
Then to the pleasant Meades did all resort.

Where as the Maides by custome came in thronges,
When any Maid was married from their traine:
And there they spend the time in sport and songs,
That other may doe so to them againe:
Where some were dancing hand in hand in ringes,
And others sit to heare how *Orpheus* sings.　　　　　　90

Here *Orpheus* warbles on his trembling stringes,
For to delight *Euridice* his joy:
She sometimes dances, then sits downe and sings,
And woman-like begins to kisse and toy,
Thus these two sporting in each others sight,
Thinkes every hower a yeare till it be night.

When as the wearie horses of the Sunne,
Began to hie them downe unto their rest,
And now their maisters journey almost done,
They end their toylsome labour in the west:　　　　　　100

Home hies these lovers with a full intent
To change these sportes to other merriment.

And as they footed ore the pleasant meades,
Like to the Huntresse, and her maiden traine:
A Serpent sliding from amongst the weeds,
Sting'd faire *Euridice*, and with that maine
Expels her ayerie Spirites from the wound,
And leaves her chill-cold body on the ground.

Nor would th'impartiall Destinies permit,
Her wofull soule to take her last adew: 110
But greedilie they seaze themselves on it,
Which downe unto the Stygian streames they drew,
Where they appointed her for to remaine,
That she might waight upon *Proserpins* traine,

Which when the Thracian Poet had perceived,
How suddainly *Euridice* was gone:
With madding furie sometimes rag'd and raved,
And then with tragicke tunes begins to mone,
Sighing that his *Eurudice* was dead,
Before she knew the pleasure of his bed.   120

And sitting there by her poysoned wound,
Saving the skarlet blood that issued foorth,
Moisture over-deare to dew the ground,
Or quench the thirst of this unsatiate earth:
Wishing or she were here with him againe,
Or he with her in the *Elizian* plaine.

Thus till pale death from her vermilion cheekes,
Had drawne the untainted mixture of her hue,
Distressed *Orpheus* with his sorrow seekes
Her now decaying beautie to renue: 130

Till when he saw that all his hope was vaine,
He tooke himselfe unto his harpe againe.

Where in a mournfull *Anteme* he bewailes
The sinister occasion of his birth:
Till his deviding voyce with teares now failes,
And cannot eccho to his other mirth:
But with sad lookes and dumbe demeanes he brings,
His countenance correspondent to his strings.

Unto whose musicke flockes the neighboring hilles,
The shadic groves, the pleasant murmuring springs,   140
And all the plaines with companie now filles,
As beasts and birds, fish, foule, and other thinges.
And when as every one had tane his seat,
Thus *Orpheus* gins his sorrowes to repeat.

You free-borne people, from inthralling bandes
Of libertie, depriving Loves estate:
Now mutually come all and joyne your handes,
And helpe your *Orpheus* to bewayle his mate.
Weepe for *Euridice* that loved me well,
Whose beauty now fades and decayes in hell.   150

Unheady rulers of this wretched clime,
You Gods I meane, whose hands directes our helme,
Why did you sort my dayes unto this time,
And in this sea of sorrow overwhelme:
The prosperous beginning of my life,
By this unjust divorcing of my wife.

Ah could your cruelty inact this deed,
To mixt sweet beauty with deformity:
For all my merites, render you this meed,
The injurious rape of my *Euridice*?   160

Shall she attend grim *Pluto* in his den,
That was belov'd of Gods, admir'd of men?

Hast thou forgot to love great *Saturnes* sonne,
Or didst thou envie *Orpheus* in his love?
Remember how thy selfe hast been orecum,
Leaving the Synode of the Gods above,
To dote on one, whose beauties greatest grace,
May not compare with sweet *Euridice* face.

Then in remembrance what thou sometime wert,
See the distrest estate wherein I am: 170
And if it rest in thee to ease my smart,
For pitie, pitie *Orpheus* miserie:
And if she have not pass'd the *Stygian* maine,
Ah, call her backe to live with me againe.

So shall thy name eterniz'd by my skill,
Be honor'd for this memorable deed:
And never shall my warbling harp be still,
But every where thy woorthinesse shall spred:
Till by my means the world resound thy power,
And thou shalt bid me cease and sing no more.   180

But if it be too late for to recall her,
And that already she hath pass'd the flood,
Where grieslie Furies, fiends, and hagges inthrall her,
Whence she can not returne to doe me good:
Then henceforth shall my strings surcease to sound,
And I will leave to sing till shee be found.

You wofull trees that witnesse of my mones,
With hanging tops and teare-distilling showes:
You silver streams, huge hils, hard rockes and stones,
That have been witnesse to my weary woes: 190

Heer all together take your last farewell,
Your *Orpheus* goes to seeke his love in hell.

And if the griesly furies will attend,
The mournfull musicke which meane time Ile make:
If *Pluto* will but suffer me to spend
Some solemne sonnets for my Loves sweet sake,
Then haply may the gentle Queene of Dis,
For pitie sake restore me to my blisse.

This said, he rous'd him from the tender grasse,
Which mourn'd in Sable to heare *Orpheus* weep   200
And in a melancholy moode doth passe,
Unto the place that leads downe to the deep,
Where was innumerable ghostes before,
Hasting for passage, downe to *Charons* shore.

And through the yrksome shadow of blacke night,
He treads the fatall way to loathsorne hell,
By many noysome vaultes depriv'd of light,
Where none but Furies, bugs, and torturs dwell.
Untill he came downe to the Stygian bankes,
Whereas the sillie ghostes attend in rankes.   210

There by the shore, poore *Orpheus* sits him down,
And gins to tune his mournfull instrument:
Whereas the soules doe flock about him soone,
To heare the sequell of this strange event.
And he with heavie lookes and countenance pale,
Recites the processe of our former tale.

Thus (quoth he) for my Love have I forsooke
The *Thracian* fieldes and company of men:
And for her sake this journey undertooke,
To ugly grim-fac'd *Plutoes* smokie den: 220

Where if I chance to meet with my delight,
These paynes will be requited with her sight.

But if I misse of my *Euridice,*
And cannot find her out amongst the fields:
Which the black judges of that monarchie,
Unto such seperated lovers yeelds,
Where they in solitarie passion spend
Their weary daies, which never shall have end.

Then will the heavie burthen of dispaire,
Clog downe my vitall spirits to the ground: 230
And my poore heart been split in two with care,
Let my poore soule escape that fatall wound.
And in that heavie plight poore *Orpheus* shall
Quite loose his comfort, labor, life and all.

By this had *Charon* landed all his freight,
And set them safe upon the other shore:
And with all speed returned thether straight,
To loade his boate againe, and carie more.
Where when he saw them clustering altogether,
Gan marveil what new ghost was then come thether.   240

But when he look'd on *Orpheus*, view'd his face,
And every circumstance had onely ey'd:
He told him that hee might not passe that place,
And to transport him flatlie he deny'd.
Had not the Poet with a pleasant straine
Quench'd the fierce furie of his wrath enflame.

Then he whose eares inur'd to heare the cries
Of painfull soules in endlesse miseries:
Whose concave feet and fierie flaming eyes,
Fixt on no subject but deformities.   250

Amaz'd to heare him stand as one that's dead,
Or chang'd to stone at sight of Gorgons head.

Such was the force of Musickes Arte in him,
As tam'd this savage brood of hellish kinde:
Enchaunted all his bodie lim by lim,
And turn'd his savage unrelenting mind.
And where before he kept him from his charge,
Now he entreats him to accept his barge.

And rowing him ore to the other side,
Curteously helps to conduct him ashore: 260
Protesting solemnly untill that tyde,
He never help'd such passengers before.

....

Whence *Orpheus* looking to the Sulphurish flame,
And foggy smokes ascending from that pit:
Oft times repeates his Lovers pleasing name,
Wishing himselfe might by her rest and sit,
Where they with Lovers songs, and sweet tun'd rime,
Might spend the course of everlasting time.   270

Then came he to the rustie gates of death,
Whereas the tripple headed porter dwels:
Who being amaz'd for to see him beneath,
Sends from his hollow throat such thundring yels,
As summon'd all the Furies at his calles,
To leaves their taskes and haste unto the walles.

Now in this place no succour doeth remayne,
To helpe him in or rid him out their clawes:
Save for to fall unto his harpe againe,
And by that meanes breake ope the brazen jawes   280

Of gredie hell, that there in darknesse holdes,
More then large heaven in his compasse folds.

Then gins the Poet tune his silver strings,
Whose heavenly harmony had power to moove:
Hilles, trees and stones, beasts, birds, and other things,
Both men on earth, and all the gods above,
To see if it would come to this event
Mongst the black people of this regiment.

You that doe triumph over Deaths successe,
And in unbaylable strong bandes detaines   290
The soules of wretched Lovers in distresse,
Tormented midst a world of endlesse paines;
For faire *Proserpines* sake, your lovelie Queene,
Heare me recite my sorrowes yet but greene.

I that amongst my Ditties woonted was
To sing the motion of eternall heaven:
How all the Planets in their circles passe,
And at their times make up their motions even.
Must change my stile, and taught by proofe to sing,
Proove the effect of Love, a fickle thing.   300

The solitarie wood which I frequented,
Wheras the Sylvan Gods admir'd my name:
Both Gods and woods together have lamented
Th'untimely proofe I tasted of the same:
And all agreeing in my tune doe sing,
How Loves effect is an unconstant thing.

The whilom desart plaines where nothing grew,
Now fertill by the meanes my musicke made:
Gin now againe for sorrow to renew
Their olde accustomable wearie trade.   310

And witnesse what a cause I have to sing,
How Loves effect is an unconstant thing.

I loved *Euridice*, the fairest face
That ever heavens eie did looke upon:
Or ever sprang from elementall race,
Or ever humaine sence were fixed on.
Whose timelesse death with teares make *Orpheus* sing,
That Loves effect is an unconstant thing.

Unconstant Lasse to him that lov'd thee well,
Made thee Commander of his lives estate: 320
To leave him so, and choose the Prince of Hell,
And thus reward his love with thankles hate.
Thy folly makes me now with sorrow sing,
The effect of Love to be a fickle thing.

Yet to regaine my losses come I heere,
To plead for mercie at grim *Plutoes* seat:
Who when he sees my waight of woes appear
And heares me all my sorrowes to repeat,
Will in his justice say, well may I sing,
That Loves effect is an unconstant thing.   330

And you the watchfull keepers of these ports,
Affoord but me the entrance to those plaines;
Where every day so many Ghosts resortes,
And I wil for requitall of your paines,
To heaven & earth, and all their creatures tell,
How gently I was entertain'd in hell.

With this the cruell Porter was content,
To give him entrance through his brazen door:
Where when he was, the Ghostes incontinent
Came flocking still about him more and more.   340

And they that whilest they liv'd had hard his songes,
For the like pleasure all of them now longes.

To whome the gentle *Thracian* not denies,
But for the better he might get his right:
With his accustomable harmonies,
He gluts their longing sences with delight:
And makes them all, both Ghostes and Furies say,
Would they might evermore heare *Orpheus* play.

Thus pleasantly they passe the foremost portch,
And now amongst the tortures enter in: 350
Where some in scalding mettall frie and scortch,
The tender superficies of their skin.
Others do freese to death, yet never die,
Whose paines and lives must last eternally.

All these and many other torturing kindes,
The force of his sweet musicke did alay:
And cheer'd againe their now dead drooping mindes,
That in these torments thus tormented stay.
And whilest he sung, forgets their former vaine,
The one his nature, th'other all his paine,   360

Then came he neere a place where hee might see,
A gliding streame, that swiftly runnes away:
Over whose bankes doth hang a broad branch'd tree,
That with much fruit her boughs to th'earth did sway.
Under whose shade in water to the chin,
Poore *Tantalus* is forc'd to labour in.

Ready to starve for food, poore soule hee standes,
And yet the fruite hangs round about his head:
But when he strives to catch them with his hand,
They are convayd from him with sudden speed.   370

And when hee hopes to quench his thirst with drinke,
Then doth the water settle downe and sinke.

By him *Ixion* on a torturing wheele,
Continually is rack'd and torne asunder:
His bodie yet decayes not any deale,
But still indures those paines, which is a woonder,
That being rack'd and tortur'd in this rate,
His bodie should continue in one state.

There lies *Promotheus* fastened to the ground,
Upon whose heart a greedy vulture feedes: 380
And wher he feeds new flesh growes in the wound,
And so his hart and hurt doe dayly breed.
And *Sisiphus* by him doth make his mone,
Wearied with labouring up the tumbling stone.

To whom when *Orpheus* came and gan to sing,
Their paines surceast, and they were something eas'd:
Whose harmonie effected such a thing,
As therwithall the Furies seem'd well pleas'd.
And all agreed there with one consent,
To spend that day in hell with merriment.   390

Then *Tantalus* his streame did run no more,
The tree hung still, and stir'd not from his head,
And he forgot the thirst he had before,
And thanked *Orpheus* for his so good deed,
In this releasing him from that paine,
Which many years before he did sustaine.

Then *Sisiphus* his rowling stone stood still:
Ixions paines began for to decrease:
Promotheus Vulture having eat her fill,
From tyring of his heart-strings gan to cease.   400

And all the tortures els that hell containes,
Did then surcease their plagues and direful paines.

And followed *Orpheus* to the Cypres trees,
Under whose shades the wearie Souldiours rest:
Who sorting there themselves in companies,
With everlasting quietnes are blest.
And in their conference there again revive
Th'exploytes they did, when as they were alive.

There was old *Priam* and his fiftie sonnes,
That for their countries honour were supprest: 410
The Greeks, whose names in every Poem runs,
There spend their quiet dayes in peace and rest.
And he whose love did win the *Carthage* Queene,
Venterous *Aeneas* rest upon that greene.

There gins the Poet once againe relate
The waightie cause that drew him to that place:
In everie word lamenting his estate,
That hee was borne to suffer this disgrace.
He that had everie creature at his call,
Should now stand need for to bee help'd of all.   420

You that have tri'd (quoth hee) Loves hard event,
And the unconstant kind of womens sect:
And you whose time in wearie warres was spent,
Which Love and Lovers passions did neglect.
For pittie sake helpe, for to cure my paine,
By getting my *Euridice* againe.

And in your judgmentes view my heavie plight,
That have adventur'd this so dangerous toyle
To view the monuments of endlesse night,
That yeelds no other thing save rape and spoyle.   430

And tell mee then, if that for all my paine,
I bee not woorthy of her love againe.

Your toyles that whilom you sustain'd above,
Was pleasure unto these I here abide:
And all your dangerous quarrels for your love,
Compar'd with mine, may all be set aside.
Yet could the world devise a greater paine,
I would endure to get my love againe.

My Love, the sweetest Love that ere survived,
Woonder of heaven, and the fame of earth: 440
Untimely death unjustly hath deprived,
And would no longer let her heare my mirth.
For her sweet sake what would I not sustaine,
If I might so recover her againe?

But your grim God detaines her from my sight,
And there remaines small meanes for to obtaine her:
Seing then she cannot be atchiv'd by might,
Then with your teares and prayers helpe to gaine her.
And see if *Pluto* pittying of your paine,
Will render my *Euridice* againe.   450

This song drew all the wandring ghosts were neere
T'attend the pitteous heavie mournfull tale:
And all of them that there were come to heare,
Joyned in one to worke for his avayle:
And towards *Pluto* all of them doe goe,
In what they could to ease the Poets woe.

To whome when as they came, *Orpheus* began,
To tell his former storie ore againe:
At whose sad tale the Furies skarslie can,
Their fierie eyes from watrie teares refraine   460

But altogether gan intreat their King,
That hee would suffer *Orpheus* but to sing.

And if his Musickes skill deserv'd so much,
As well they knew it could obtaine no lesse:
For that nor heaven, nor earth affoord none such,
As could such heavenly harmony expresse.
That he would then in recompence of this,
Restore him once again unto his blisse.

Then *Pluto* willing for to heare him play,
Calles *Proserpine* and all her maiden-train: 470
And then the Thracian gins for to assay,
What musicke he might make to please their vaine.
And somewhat doubtfull how he might begin,
At length he boldly thus begins to sing.

Ye princely Nymphes of *Helicon*,
In musicke first before the rest:
You that *Apollo* doted on,
And happy soules with knowledge blest,
Now come and help me sing and play,
Quod Amor vincit omnia.   480

And let my songs worke such effect,
And molifie this angrie King:
That he might not my rimes reject,
And scornfullie refuse this thing,
But chaunted foorth with notes may say,
Quod Amor vincit omnia.

Thou great Commaunder of this Court,
Triumphant victor over death:
To whom so manie soules resort,
When pale-fac'd death gins stop their breath: 490

Witnesse the trueth of this I say,
Quod Amor vincit omnia.

When for thy Love thou didst ore-passe
The fatall pitchie-Stygian brooke:
And came to Ceres, where she was,
And from her mother there her tooke,
Then didst thou sing what now I play,
Quod Amor vincit omnia.

And in regard what thou wert then,
A Captive unto conquering Love.   500
Pittie the poore estate of men,
And let my sorrowes somewhat moove.
Come beare a parte with mee and say,
Quod Amor vincit omnia.

For Love thy brother *Jove* forsooke,
His glorious high celestial seate:
And to a Peere himselfe betooke,
That with his *Danea* hee might treat
And did himselfe confesse and say,
Quod Amor vincit omina.   510

Apollo, Learnings greatest friend,
For *Daphnes* sake came from above:
And doted on her, to this end
He might on earth enjoy her love.
And was the first that ere did say,
Quod Amor vincit omnia.

Thus Love that enters at the eie,
And sleely steales downe to the heart:
There doth ingender fantasie,

Whose issue breeds, or joy, or smart.   520
Perforce enforces all to say,
Quod Amor vincit omnia.

This fancie hath set me on fire,
And furiously inflames my breast:
Feeding my Soule with fierce desire
Of her whose thought denies me rest.
And makes me sing both night and day,
Quod Amor vincit omnia.

Whose faire *Idea* thou hast got,
To beare *Proserpine* companie: 530
Keeping her close that I might not
Looke on my faire *Euridice.*
Which now with sorrow makes me say,
Quod Amor vincit omnia.

Shee stands thee heere in little steed,
For thou hast many Millions more:
Then with her love supply my need,
And I will sing thy praise therfore.
And whilest I live still will I say,
Quod Amor vincit omnia.   540

Plead faire *Proserpine* for her sake,
Who in her prime of love decay'd
And on her some compassion take,
Which was a wife, yet di'd a maid.
For thou knowst well what joy is bred
Enjoying of a Lovers bed.

Fortune and Love unconstant friends,
Agreed unto our marriage day:
And furdred all our Loves pretends,
With what within their power lay: 550
Untill we had both woo'd and wed,
Then Fortune snach'd her from my bed.

And in despight of Love detaines,
Euridice within your power:
And me afflictes with Lovers paines,
Which are increasing everie hower.
Because she knew not what was bred
Within a Lovers loyall bed.

In that inclosure breeds delight,
The pleasing soule of sweet content: 560
Contented best to spend the night,
In such soule-pleasing merriment.
As thou canst witnesse well, is bred
Within a loyall Lovers bed.

Where all *Elizian* joyes doe dwell,
Incircled there by *Cupids* charmes,
And more delight then I can tell,
Ingendred in a Lovers armes.
Because I tried not what was bred,
Within a loyall Lovers bed.   570

But that instinct of Nature tels,
The hidden pleasure of that place:
Where more delightsome daliance dwels,
Then in the gazing on her face.
There are the livelie pleasures bred,
That longs unto a mariage bed.

Of this faire marke did *Orpheus* misse,
And lost the pleasure of that sport:
Been come unto the gates of blisse,
I could not get into the fort: 580
For my *Euridice* was dead,
Before I could enjoy her bed.

With this the Poet over-cloyd with griefe,
No further could extend his miserie:
But with sad teares seem'd to implore reliefe,
To rid him from this wofull extasie,
At whose sad teares the fearful god did grant
That he should have her with this covenant.

In all his wearie journey up againe,
Hee should not once looke backe unto his love: 590
But from the speaking to her should refraine,
Untill he came up to the world above,
Which if he did, then should he all his life,
Enjoy her bodie as his married wife.

But if fond jealousie should make him doubt,
And he looke backe to see his Loves sweet face:
Before he were from his vast kingdome out,
And past the fatall limmits of that place.
Then should his wife be snatch'd away againe,
And he should nere the like good turne obtaine.   600

Which curtesie the Poet gentlie tooke,
And with contentment did accept this thing
Expecting her with manie a lingring looke,
The cause that drew him thether for to sing.
Till at the length as the grim-God commands,
Euridice was rendred to his hands.

But intercourse of speech was there forbidden,
He might not welcome her with loving words:
And with a duskie vale her face was hidden,
That no transparance from her eies affoords.   610
He was commanded to eschue the place,
And she had leave to follow him apace.

Thus both together these two Lovers goe,
With this restraint of mutuall conference:
Whose sad demeanes the witnesses of woe,
Shew'd discontent, but that with patience
Men must of force obey the Gods decrees,
Though they extend unto their injuries.

Long thus they traveill'd in this discontent,
Each wishing of the other to have sight: 620
Untill their journey now was almost spent,
And they might see a glimmering of the light:
For they were wel-nigh come unto those bounds,
That parts *Avernus* and the upper grounds,

Where jealous thought that in a restlesse mind,
Breeds discontented passions mixt with feare:
Was urging *Orpheus* oft to looke behind,
To see if his *Euridice* were there,
Untill remembrance of his promise tolde,
He might not venter for to be so bold.   630

Oft was his faltring tongue about to speake,
And call his sweetest Love by her sweet name:
But being halfe afrayd least he should breake
The Gods behests, and so incurre his shame:
With much adoe his speaking doth refraine:
Although (God knowes) it was unto his paine.

But longer can he not forbeare to see,
If shee did follow him along or no:
Such was th'effect of burning jealousie,
That would not let him any further goe,   640
Before he had satisfi'd his longing mind,
In looking if his lover were behind.

And at the length boldly assayes to trie,
Turning him backe to her, whom he so loved:
When she was snatched from him by and by
And from his sight immediatly remooved.
And he himselfe left to himselfe againe,
Because he did not from this thing refraine.

Grieving to see himselfe thus overshot,
And all his labour sort unto that end: 650
Leaving that cursed place, he homward got,
There fullie bending of himselfe to spend
The future remnant of his single life,
In scorne of pleasing Love, or loving wife.

And in invective Ditties daylie singes,
Th'uncertain pleasure of unconstant Love:
How manie woes a womans beautie bringes
And into what extreames this joy doth shove
Poore follish men, that ere they be awarre
Will rashlie overshoot themselves so farre.   660

There gins he sing of secrete Loves deceites,
And womens fawning fickle companie:
The outward golden shew of poysoned baytes,
That drawes so many men to miserie.
And for an instance sets himselfe to shew,
One that had suffred all this pleasing woe.

Whose songes did sort unto such deepe effect,
As draw mens fancies from thir former wives:
Womens vaine love beginning to neglect.
And in the fields with *Orpheus* spend their lives: 670
With which sweet life they seem'd so well content,
As made them curse the former time the'ad spent.

At which the women not a little grieve,
To see their conquering Captaine thus ore-borne:
They gin devise how best they might relieve,
Their fading glorie being almost worne.
Which by no meanes they hope for to atchieue,
As long as *Orpheus* doth remaine alive.

Which to prevent in solemne wise they cite,
Their companie together all in one: 680
Where everie busie head will needs indite,
A meanes how they might get poore *Orpheus* gone,
Mongst whome at length the case was thus derived,
That *Orpheus* of his life should be deprived.

And thus they all agreed in one consent,
By some occasion to procure his end:
When to the place they flocke incontinent,
Whereas he us'd his wofull dayes to spend,
And finding him alone without his traine,
Upon him fall they all with might and maine.   690

And with confused weapons beat him downe,
Quenching their angrie thirst with his warm blood:
At whose untimely death though heavens frowne,
Yet they defend their quarrell to be good,
And for their massacre this reason render,
He was an enemie unto their gender.

Which done, to rid him quite out of the way,
Him and his Harpe they into *Hebar* fling:
Upon whose stringes the gliding streames doe play,
And for his soule lamenting Dirges sing   700
Till to the watrie Oceans greedy wombe,
They carie him for to go seeke his tombe.

But then faire heauens in their due regard,
Pittying his end that so had spent his dayes:
In justice thus his merits do reward,
Unto their ever memorable praise.
Thus they determin'd all with one consent,
For to draw up his heavenlie Instrument.

And place it in that Christall monument,
The everliving registrie of fame: 710
The golden starrie-spangled firmament,
Where in remembrance of the Poets name
Stands *Lyra* to renue his memorie,
Whose endlesse date out-lives eternitie.

FINIS.

The Affectionate Shepheard.

Containing the Complaint of Daphnis for the love of Ganymede.

Amor plus mellis, quam fellis, est.

London,
Printed by John Danter for T.G. and E.N.
and are to bee sold in Saint Dunstones
Church-yeard in Fleetstreet,
1594.

To the Right Excellent
and most beautiful Lady,
the Ladie Penelope Ritch.

Fayre lovely Ladie, whose Angelique eyes
Are Vestall Candles of sweet Beauties Treasure,
Whose speech is able to inchaunt the wise,
Converting Joy to Paine, and Paine to Pleasure;
Accept this simple Toy of my Soules Dutie,
Which I present unto thy matchles Beautie,

And albeit the gift be all too meane,
Too meane an Offring for thine Ivorie Shrine;
Yet must thy Beautie my just blame susteane,
Since it is mortall, but thy selfe divine.
Then (Noble Ladie) take in gentle worth,
This new-borne Babe which here my Muse brings forth.

Your Honours most affectionate
and perpetually devoted Shepheard:

DAPHNIS.

The Teares of an affectionate Shepheard
sicke for Love.
or
The Complaint of *Daphnis*
for the Love of *Ganimede,*

Scarce had the morning Starre hid from the light
Heavens crimson Canopie with stars bespangled,
But I began to rue th'unhappy sight
Of that faire Boy that had my hart intangled;
Cursing the Time, the Place, the sense, the sin;
I came, I saw, I viewd, I slipped in.

If it be sinne to love a sweet-fac'd Boy,
(Whose amber locks trust up in golden tramels
Dangle adowne his lovely cheekes with joy,
When pearle and flowers his faire haire enamels)   10
If it be sinne to love a lovely Lad;
Oh then sinne I, for whom my soule is sad.

His Ivory-white and Alablaster skin
Is staind throughout with rare Vermillion red,
Whose twinckling starrie lights do never blin
To shine on lovely *Venus* (Beauties bed:)
But as the Lillie and the blushing Rose,
So white and red on him in order growes.

Upon a time the Nymphs bestird them-selves
To trie who could his beautie soonest win: 20
But he accounted them but all as Elves,
Except it were the faire Queene *Guendolen,*
Her he embrac'd, of her was beloved,
With plaints he proved, and with teares he moved.

But her an Old-Man had beene sutor too,
That in his age began to doate againe;
Her would he often pray, and often woo,
When through old-age enfeebled was his Braine:
But she before had lov'd a lustie youth
That now was dead, the cause of all her ruth.   30

And thus it hapned, Death and *Cupid* met
Upon a time at swilling *Bacchus* house,
Where daintie cates upon the Boord were set,
And Goblets full of wine to drinke carouse:
Where Love and Death did love the licor so,
That out they fall and to the fray they goe.

And having both their Quivers at their backe
Fild full of Arrows; Th'one of fatall steele,
The other all of gold; Deaths shaft was black,
But Loves was yellow: Fortune turnd her wheele;   40
And from Deaths Quiver fell a fatall shaft,
That under *Cupid* by the winde was waft.

And at the same time by ill hap there fell
Another Arrow out of *Cupids* Quiver;
The which was carried by the winde at will,
And under Death the amorous shaft did shiver:
They being parted, Love tooke up Deaths dart,
And Death tooke up Loves Arrow (for his part.)

Thus as they wandred both about the world,
At last Death met with one of feeble age: 50
Wherewith he drew a shaft and at him hurld
The unknowne Arrow; (with a furious rage)
Thinking to strike him dead with Deaths blacke dart,
But he (alas) with Love did wound his hart.

This was the doting foole, this was the man
That lovd faire *Guendolena* Queene of Beautie;
Shee cannot shake him off, doo what she can,
For he hath vowd to her his soules last duety:
Making him trim upon the holy-daies;
And crownes his Love with Garlands made of Baies.   60

Now doth he stroke his Beard; and now (againe)
He wipes the drivel from his filthy chin;
Now offers he a kisse; but high Disdaine
Will not permit her hart to pity him:
Her hart more hard than Adamant or steele,
Her hart more changeable than Fortunes wheele.

But leave we him in love (up to the eares)
And tell how Love behav'd himselfe abroad;
Who seeing one that mourned still in teares
(A young-man groaning under Loves great Load)   70
Thinking to ease his Burden, rid his paines:
For men have griefe as long as life remaines.

Alas (the while) that unawares he drue
The fatall shaft that Death had dropt before;
By which deceit great harme did then insue,
Stayning his face with blood and filthy goare.
His face, that was to *Guendolen* more deere
Than love of Lords, or any lordly Peere.

This was that fair and beautifull young-man,   80
Whom *Guendolena* so lamented for;
This is that Love whom she doth curse and ban,
Because she doth that dismall chaunce abhor:
And if it were not for his Mothers sake,
Even *Ganimede* himselfe she would forsake.

Oh would shee would forsake my *Ganimede,*
Whose sugred love is full of sweete delight,
Upon whose fore-head you may plainely reade
Loves Pleasure, grav'd in yvorie Tables bright:
In whose faire eye-balls you may clearely see
Base Love still staind with foule indignitie.   90

Oh would to God he would but pitty mee,
That love him more than any mortall wight;
Then he and I with love would soone agree,
That now cannot abide his Sutors sight.
O would to God (so I might have my fee)
My lips were honey, and thy mouth a Bee.

Then shouldst thou sucke my sweete and my faire flower
That now is ripe, and full of honey-berries:
Then would I leade thee to my pleasant Bower
Fild full of Grapes, of Mulberries, and Cherries;   100
Then shouldst thou be my Waspe or else my Bee,
I would thy hive, and thou my honey bee.

I would put amber Bracelets on thy wrests,
Crownets of Pearle about thy naked Armes:
And when thou sitst at swilling *Bacchus* feasts
My lips with charmes should save thee from all harmes:
And when in sleepe thou tookst thy chiefest Pleasure,
Mine eyes should gaze upon thine eye-lids Treasure.

And every Morne by dawning of the day,
When *Phoebus* riseth with a blushing face,   110
Silvanus Chappel-Clarkes shall chaunt a Lay,
And play thee hunts-up in thy resting place:
My Coote thy Chamber, my bosome thy Bed,
Shall be appointed for thy sleepy head.

And when it pleaseth thee to walke abroad,
(Abroad into the fields to take fresh ayre:)
The Meades with *Floras* treasure should be strowde,
(The mantled meaddowes and the fields so fayre.)
And by a silver Well (with golden sands)
Ile sit me downe, and wash thine yvory hands.   120

And in the sweltring heate of summer time,
I would make Cabinets for thee (my Love:)
Sweet smelling Arbours made of Eglantine
Should be thy shrine, and I would be thy Dove.
Coole Cabinets of fresh greene Laurell boughs
Should shadow us, ore-set with thicke-set Eughes.

Or if thou list to bathe thy naked limbs,
Within the Christall of a Pearle-bright brooke,
Paved with dainty pibbles to the brims;
Or cleare, wherein thy selfe thy selfe mayst looke;   130
Weele goe to *Ladon*, whose still trickling noyse,
Will lull thee fast asleepe amids thy joyes.

Or if thoult goe unto the River side,
To angle for the sweet fresh-water fish;
Arm'd with thy implements that will abide
(Thy rod, hooke, line) to take a dainty dish;
Thy rods shall be of cane, thy lines of silke,
Thy hooks of silver, and thy bayts of milke.

Or if thou lov'st to heare sweet Melodie,
Or pipe a Round upon an Oaten Reede,   140
Or make thy selfe glad with some myrthfull glee,
Or play them Musicke whilst thy flocke doth feede;
To *Pans* owne Pype Ile helpe my lovely Lad,
(*Pans* golden Pype) which he of *Syrinx* had.

Or if thou dar'st to climbe the highest Trees
For Apples, Cherries, Medlars, Peares, or Plumbs,
Nuts, Walnuts, Filbeards, Chest-nuts, Cervices,
The hoary Peach, when snowy winter comes;
I have fine Orchards full of mellowed frute;
Which I will give thee to obtain my sute.   150

Not proud *Alcynous* himselfe can vaunt,
Of goodlier Orchards or of braver Trees
Than I have planted; yet thou wilt not graunt
My simple sute; but like the honey Bees
Thou suckst the flowre till all the sweet be gone;
And lov'st mee, for my Coyne till I have none.

Leave *Guendolen* (sweet hart) though she be faire
Yet is she light; not light in vertue shining:
But light in her behaviour, to impaire
Her honour in her Chastities declining;   160
Trust not her tears, for they can wantonnize,
When teares in pearle are trickling from her eyes.

If thou wilt come and dwell with me at home;
My sheep-cote shall be strowd with new greene rushes:
Weele haunt the trembling Prickets as they rome
About the fields, along the hauthorne bushes;
I have a pie-bald Curre to hunt the Hare:
So we will live with daintie forrest fare.

Nay more than this, I have a Garden-plot,
Wherein there wants nor hearbs, nor roots, nor flowers;   170
(Flowers to smell, roots to eate, hearbs for the pot,)
And dainty Shelters when the Welkin lowers:
Sweet-smelling Beds of Lillies and of Roses,
Which Rosemary banks and Lavender incloses.

There growes the Gilliflowre, the Mynt, the Dayzie
(Both red and white,) the blew-veynd-Violet:
The purple Hyacinth, the Spyke to please thee,
The scarlet dyde Carnation bleeding yet;
The Sage, the Savery, and sweet Margerum,
Isop, Tyme, and Eye-bright, good for the blinde and dumbe.   180

The Pinke, the Primrose, Cowslip, and Daffadilly,
The Hare-bell blue, the crimson Cullumbine,
Sage, Lettis, Parsley, and the milke-white Lilly,
The Rose, and speckled flowre cald Sops in wine,
Fine pretie King-cups, and the yellow Bootes,
That growes by Rivers, and by shallow Brookes.

And manie thousand moe (I cannot name)
Of hearbs and flowers that in gardens grow,
I have for thee; and Coneyes that be tame,
Yong Rabbets, white as Swan, and blacke as Crow,   190
Some speckled here and there with daintie spots:
And more I have two mylch and milke-white Goates.

All these, and more, Ile give thee for thy love;
If these, and more, may tyce thy love away:
I have a Pidgeon-house, in it a Dove,
Which I love more than mortall tongue can say:
And last of all, Ile give thee a little Lambe
To play withall, new weaned from her Dam.

But if thou wilt not pittie my Complaint,
My teares, nor Vowes, nor Oathes, made to thy Beautie;   200
What shall I doo? But languish, die, or faint,
Since thou dost scorne my Teares, and my Soules Duetie:
And Teares contemned, Vowes and Oaths must faile;
For where Teares cannot, nothing can prevaile.

Compare the love of faire Queene *Guendolin*
With mine, and thou shalt see how she doth love thee:
I love thee for thy qualities divine,
But Shee doth love another Swaine above thee:
I love thee for thy gifts, She for hir pleasure;
I for thy Vertue, She for Beauties treasure.   210

And alwaies (I am sure) it cannot last,
But sometime Nature will denie those dimples:
In steed of Beautie (when thy Blossom's past)
Thy face will be deformed, full of wrinckles:
Then She that lov'd thee for thy Beauties sake,
When Age drawes on, thy love will soone forsake.

But I that lov'd thee for thy gifts divine,
In the December of thy Beauties waning,
Will still admire (with joy) those lovely eine,
That now behold me with their beauties baning: 220
Though Januarie will never come againe,
Yet Aprill yeres will come in showers of raine.

When will my May come, that I may embrace thee?
When will the hower be of my soules joying?
Why dost thou seeke in mirthe still to disgrace mee?
Whose mirth's my health, whose griefe's my harts annoying.
Thy bane my bale, thy blisse my blessednes,
Thy ill my hell, thy weale my welfare is.

Thus doo I honour thee that love thee so,
And love thee so, that so doo honour thee,   230
Much more than anie mortall man doth know,
Or can discerne by Love or jealozie:

But if that thou disdainst my loving ever;
Oh happie I, if I had loved never.

Plus fellis quam mellis Amor.

The Second Dayes Lamentation
of the *Affectionate Shepheard.*

Next Morning when the golden Sunne was risen,
And new had bid good morrow to the Mountaines;
When Night her silver light had lockt in prison,
Which gave a glimmering on the christall Fountaines:
Then ended sleepe: and then my cares began,
Ev'n with the uprising of the silver Swan.

O glorious Sunne quoth I, (viewing the Sunne)
That lightenst everie thing but me alone:
Why is my Summer season almost done?
My Spring-time past, and Ages Autumne gone?   10
My Harvest's come, and yet I reapt no corne:
My love is great, and yet I am forlorne.

Witnes these watrie eyes my sad lament,
(Receaving cisternes of my ceaseles teares),
Witnes my bleeding hart my soules intent,
Witnes the weight distressed *Daphnis* beares:
Sweet Love, come ease me of thy burthens paine;
Or els I die, or else my hart is slaine.

And thou love-scorning Boy, cruell, unkinde;   20
Oh let me once againe intreat some pittie:
May be thou wilt relent thy marble minde,

And lend thine eares unto my dolefull Dittie:
Oh pittie him, that pittie craves so sweetly;
Or else thou shalt be never named meekly.

If thou wilt love me, thou shalt be my Boy,
My sweet Delight, the Comfort of my minde,
My Love, my Dove, my Sollace, and my Joy:
But if I can no grace nor mercie finde,
Ile goe to *Caucasus* to ease my smart,
And let a Vulture gnaw upon my hart.   30

Yet if thou wilt but show me one kinde looke,
(A small reward for my so great affection)
Ile grave thy name in Beauties golden Booke,
And shrowd thee under *Hellicons* protection;
Making the Muses chaunt thy lovely prayse:
(For they delight in Shepheards lowly layes.)

And when th'art wearie of thy keeping Sheepe
Upon a lovely Downe, (to please thy minde)
Ile give thee fine ruffe-footed Doves to keepe,
And pretie Pidgeons of another kinde: 40
A Robbin-red-brest shall thy Minstrell bee,
Chirping thee sweet, and pleasant Melodie.

Or if thou wilt goe shoote at little Birds
With bow and boult, (the Thrustle-cocke and Sparrow)
Such as our Countrey hedges can afford's;
I have a fine bowe, and an yvorie arrow:
And if thou Misse, yet meate thou shalt not lacke,
Ile hang a bag and a bottle at thy backe.

Wilt thou set springes in a frostie Night,
To catch the long-billd Woodcocke and the Snype?   50
(By the bright glimmering of the Starrie light)
The Partridge, Phaesant, or the greedie Grype?
Ile lend thee lyme-twigs, and fine sparrow calls,
Wherewith the Fowler silly Birds inthralls.

Or in a mystie morning if thou wilt
Make pit-falls for the Larke and Pheldifare;
Thy prop and sweake shall be both over-guilt:
With *Cyparissus* selfe thou shalt compare
For gins and wyles, the Oozels to beguile;
Whilst thou under a bush shalt sit and smile.   60

Or with Hare-pypes (set in a muset hole)
Wilt thou deceave the deep-earth-delving Coney?
Or wilt thou in a yellow Boxen bole
Taste with a woodden splent the sweet lythe honey?
Clusters of crimson Grapes Ile pull thee downe;
And with Vine-leaves make thee a lovely Crowne.

Or wilt thou drinke a cup of new-made Wine
Froathing at top, mixt with a dish of Creame;
And Straw-berries, or Bil-berries in their prime,
Bath'd in a melting Sugar-Candie streame: 70
Bunnell and Perry I have for thee (alone)
When Vynes are dead, and all the Grapes are gone.

I have a pleasant noted Nightingale,
That sings as sweetly as the silver Swan)
Kept in a Cage of bone; as white as Whale,
Which I with singing of *Philemon* wan:

Her shalt thou have, and all I have beside
If thou wilt be my Boy, or else my Bride.

Then will I lay out all my Lardarie
(Of Cheese, of Cracknells, Curds and Clowted-creame)   80
Before thy male-content ill-pleasing eye:
But why doo I of such great follies dreame?
Alas, he will not see my simple Coate;
For all my speckled Lambe, nor milk-white Goat.

Against my Birth-day thou shalt be my guest:
Weele have Greene-cheeses, and fine Silly-bubs;
And thou shalt be the chiefe of all my feast.
And I will give thee two fine pretie Cubs,
With two Young Whelps, to make thee sport withall,
A golden Racket, and a Tennis-ball.   90

A guilded Nutmeg, and a race of Ginger,
A silken Girdle, and a drawn-worke Band,
Cuffs for thy wrists, a gold Ring for thy finger,
And sweet Rose-water for thy Lilly-white hand,
A Purse of silke, bespangd with spots of gold,
As brave a one as ere thou didst behold.

A paire of Knives, a greene Hat and a Feather,
New Gloves to put upon thy milk-white hand
Ile give thee, for to keep thee from the weather;
With Phoenix feathers shall thy Face be fand,   100
Cooling those Cheeks, that being cool'd wexe red,
Like Lillyes in a bed of Roses shed.

Why doo thy Corall lips disdaine to kisse,
And sucke that Sweete, which manie have desired?
That Baulme my Bane, that meanes would mend my misse:
Oh let me then with thy sweete Lips b'inspired;
When thy Lips touch my Lips, my Lips will turne
To Corall too, and being cold yce will burne.

Why should thy sweet Love-locke hang dangling downe,
Kissing thy girdle-steed with falling pride?   110
Although thy Skin be white, thy haire is browne:
Oh let not then thy haire thy beautie hide;
Cut off thy Locke, and sell it for gold wier:
(The purest gold is tryde in hottest fier).

Faire-long-haire-wearing *Absolon* was kild,
Because he wore it in a braverie:
So that whiche gracde his Beautie, Beautie spild,
Making him subject to vile slaverie,
In being hangd: a death for him too good,
That sought his owne shame, and his Fathers blood.   120

Againe, we read of old King *Priamus*,
(The haplesse syre of valiant *Hector* slaine)
That his haire was so long and odious
In youth, that in his age it bred his paine:
For if his haire had not been halfe so long,
His life had been, and he had had no wrong.

For when his stately Citie was destroyd,
(That Monument of great Antiquitie)
When his poore hart (with griefe and sorrow cloyd)
Fled to his Wife (last hope in miserie;)   130

Pyrrhus (more hard than Adamantine rockes)
Held him and halde him by his aged lockes.

These two examples by the way I show,
To prove th'indecencie of mens long haire:
Though I could tell thee of a thousand moe,
Let these suffice for thee (my lovely Faire)
Whose eye's my starre; whose smiling is my Sunne;
Whose love did ende before my joyes begunne.

Fond Love is blinde, and so art thou (my Deare)
For thou seest not my Love, and great desart;   140
Blinde Love is fond, and so thou dost appeare;
For fond, and blinde, thou greevst my greeving hart:
Be thou fond-blinde, blinde-fond, or one, or all;
Thou art my Love, and I must be thy thrall.

Oh lend thine yvorie fore-head for Loves Booke,
Thine eyes for candles to behold the same;
That when dim-sighted ones therein shall looke
They may discerne that proud disdainefull Dame;
Yet claspe that Booke, and shut that Cazement light;
Lest th'one obscurde, the other shine too bright.   150

Sell thy sweet breath to'th'daintie Musk-ball-makers;
Yet sell it so as thou mayst soone redeeme it:
Let others of thy beauty be pertakers;
Els none but *Daphnis* will so well esteeme it:
For what is Beauty except it be well knowne?
And how can it be knowne, except first showne?

Learne of the Gentlewomen of this Age,
That set their Beauties to the open view,
Making Disdaine their Lord, true Love their Page;
A Custome Zeale doth hate, Desert doth rue: 160
Learne to looke red, anon waxe pale and wan,
Making a mocke of Love, a scorne of man.

A candle light, and cover'd with a vaile,
Doth no man good, because it gives no light;
So beauty of her beauty seemes to faile,
When being not seene it cannot shine so bright.
Then show thy selfe and know thy selfe withall,
Lest climing high thou catch too great a fall.

Oh foule Eclipser of that fayre sun-shine,
Which is intitled Beauty in the best;   170
Making that mortall, which is els divine,
That staines the fayre which Women steeme not least:
Get thee to Hell againe (from whence thou art)
And leave the Center of a Woman's hart.

Ah be not staind (sweet Boy) with this vilde spot,
Indulgence Daughter, Mother of mischaunce;
A blemish that doth every beauty blot;
That makes them loath'd, but never doth advaunce
Her Clyents, fautors, friends; or them that love her;
And hates them most of all, that most reprove her.   180

Remember Age, and thou canst not be prowd,
For age puls downe the pride of every man;
In youthfull yeares by Nature tis allowde
To have selfe-will, doo Nurture what she can;

Nature and Nurture once together met,
The Soule and shape in decent order set.

Pride looks aloft, still staring on the starres,
Humility looks lowly on the ground;
Th'one menaceth the Gods with civill warres,
The other toyles til he have Vertue found: 190
His thoughts are humble, not aspiring hye;
But Pride looks haughtily with scornefull eye.

Humillity is clad in modest weedes,
But Pride is brave and glorious to the show;
Humillity his friends with kindnes feedes,
But Pride his friends (in neede) will never know:
Supplying not their wants, but them disdaining;
Whilst they to pitty never neede complayning.

Humillity in misery is reliev'd,
But Pride in neede of no man is regarded;   200
Pitty and Mercy weepe to see him griev'd
That in distress had them so well rewarded:
But Pride is scornd, contemnd, disdaind, derided,
Whilst Humblenes of all things is provided.

Oh then be humble, gentle, meeke, and milde;
So shalt thou be of every mouth comended;
Be not disdainful, cruell, proud, (sweet childe)
So shalt thou be of no man much condemned;
Care not for them that Vertue doo despise;
Vertue is loathde of fooles; lovde of the wise.   210

O faire Boy trust not to thy Beauties wings,
They cannot carry thee above the Sunne:
Beauty and wealth are transitory things,
(For all must ende that ever was begunne)
But Fame and Vertue never shall decay;
For Fame is toombles, Vertue lives for aye.

The snow is white, and yet the pepper's blacke,
The one is bought, the other is contemned: 220
Pibbles we have, but store of Jeat we lacke;
So white comparde to blacke is much condemned:
We doo not praise the Swanne because shees white,
But for she doth in Musique much delite.

And yet the silver-noted Nightingale,
Though she be not so white is more esteemed;
Sturgion is dun of hew, white is the Whale,
Yet for the daintier Dish the first is deemed;
What thing is whiter than the milke-bred Lilly?
Thou knowes it not for naught, what man so silly?

Yea what more noysomer unto the smell
Than Lillies are? what's sweeter than the Sage?   230
Yet for pure white the Lilly beares the Bell
Till it be faded through decaying Age;
House-Doves are white, and Oozels Blacke-birds bee;
Yet what a difference in the taste, we see.

Compare the Cow and Calfe, with Ewe and Lambe;
Rough hayrie Hydes, with softest downy Fell;
Hecfar and Bull, with Weather and with Ramme,
And you shall see how far they doo excell;

White Kine with blacke, blacke Coney-skins with gray,
Kine, nesh and strong; skins, deare and cheape alway.　　　　240

The whitest silver is not alwaies best,
Lead, Tynne, and Pewter are of base esteeme;
The yellow burnisht gold, that comes from th'East,
And West (of late invented) may beseeme
The worlds ritch Treasury, or *Mydas* eye;
(The Ritch mans God, poore mans felicitie.)

Bugle and Jeat, with snow and Alablaster
I will compare: White Dammasin with blacke;
Bullas and wheaton Plumbs, (to a good Taster,)
The ripe red Cherries have the sweetest smacke;　　　　250
When they be greene and young, th'are sowre and naught;
But being ripe, with eagerness th'are baught.

Compare the Wyld-cat to the brownish Beaver,
Running for life, with hounds pursued sore;
When Hunts-men of her pretious Stones bereave her
(Which with her teeth sh'had bitten off before):
Restoratives, and costly curious Felts
Are made of them, and rich imbroydred Belts.

To what use serves a peece of crimbling Chalke?
The Agget stone is white, yet good for nothing:　　　　260
Fie, fie, I am asham'd to heare thee talke;
Be not so much of thine owne Image doating:
So faire Narcissus lost his love and life.
(Beautie is often with itselfe at strife).

Right Diamonds are of a russet hieu,
The brightsome Carbuncles are red to see too,
The Saphyre stone is of a watchet blue,
(To this thou canst not chuse but soone agree too):
Pearles are not white but gray, Rubies are red:
In praise of Blacke, what can be better sed?   270

For if we doo consider of each thing
That flyes in welkin, or in water swims,
How everie thing increaseth with the Spring,
And how the blacker still the brighter dims:
We cannot chuse, but needs we must confesse,
Sable excels milk-white in more or lesse.

As for example, in the christall cleare
Of a sweete streame, or pleasant running River,
Where thousand formes of fishes will appeare,
(Whose names to thee I cannot now deliver:)   280
The blacker still the brighter have disgrac'd,
For pleasant profit, and delicious taste.

Salmon and Trout are of a ruddie colour,
Whiting and Dare is of a milk-white hiew:
Nature by them (Perhaps) is made the fuller,
Little they nourish, be they old or new:
Carp, Loach, Tench, Eeles (though black and bred in mud)
Delight the tooth with taste, and breed good blud.

Innumerable be the kindes, if I could name them;
But I a Shepheard, and no Fisher am: 290
Little it skills whether I praise or blame them,
I onely meddle with my Ew and Lamb:

Yet this I say, that blacke the better is,
In birds, beasts, frute, stones, flowres, herbs, mettals, fish.

And last of all, in blacke there doth appeare
Such qualities, as not in yvorie;
Black cannot blush for shame, looke pale for fear,
Scorning to weare another livorie.
Blacke is the badge of sober Modestie,
The wonted weare of ancient Gravetie.   300

The learned Sisters sute themselves in blacke,
Learning abandons white, and lighter hues:
Pleasure and Pride light colours never lacke;
But true Religion doth such Toyes refuse:
Vertue and Gravity are sisters growne,
Since blacke by both, and both by blacke are knowne.

White is the colour of each paltry Miller,
White is the Ensigne of each common Woman;
White, is white Vertues for blacke Vyces Piller;
White makes proud fooles inferiour unto no man: 310
White, is the white of Body, blacke of Minde,
(Vertue we seldome in white Habit finde.)

On then be not so proud because th'art fayre,
Vertue is onely the ritch gift of God:
Let not selfe-pride thy vertues name impayre,
Beate not greene youth with sharpe Repentance Rod:
(A Fiend, a Monster, a mishapen Divel;
Vertues foe, Vyces friend, the roote of evill.)

Apply thy minde to be a vertuous man,
Avoyd ill company (the spoyle of youth;)   320
To follow Vertues Lore doo what thou can,
(Whereby great profit unto thee ensuth:)
Reade Bookes, hate Ignorance, (the Foe to Art,
The Damme of Errour, Envy of the hart.)

Serve *Jove* (upon thy knees) both day and night,
Adore his Name above all things on Earth:
So shall thy vowes be gracious in his sight,
So little Babes are blessed in their Birth:
Thinke on no worldly woe, lament thy sin;
(For lesser cease, when greater griefes begin).   330

Sweare no vaine oathes; heare much, but little say;
Speake ill of no man, tend thine owne affaires,
Bridle thy wrath, thine angrie moode delay;
(So shall thy minde be seldome cloyd with cares:)
Be milde and gentle in thy speech to all,
Refuse no honest gaine when it doth fall.

Be not beguild with words, prove not ungratefull,
Releeve thy Neighbour in his greatest need,
Commit no action that to all is hatefull,
Their want with welth, the poore with plentie feed: 340
Twit no man in the teeth with what th'hast done;
Remember flesh is fraile, and hatred shunne.

Leave wicked things, which Men to mischiefe move,
(Least crosse mis-hap may thee in danger bring,)
Crave no preferment of thy heavenly *Jove,*
Nor anie honor of thy earthly King:

Boast not thy selfe before th'Almighties sight,
(Who knowes thy hart, and anie wicked wight).

Be not offensive to the peoples eye,
See that thy praiers harts true zeale affords,   350
Scorne not a man that's falne in miserie,
Esteeme no tatling tales, nor babling words;
That reason is exiled alwaies thinke,
When as a drunkard rayles amidst his drinke.

Use not thy lovely lips to loathsome lyes,
By craftie means increase no worldly wealth;
Strive not with mightie Men (whose fortune flies)
With temp'rate diet nourish wholesome health:
Place well thy words, leave not thy frend for gold;
First trie, then trust; in ventring be not bold.   360

In *Pan* repose thy trust; extoll his praise
(That never shall decay, but ever lives):
Honor thy Parents (to prolong thy dayes),
Let not thy left hand know what right hand gives:
From needie men turn not thy face away,
(Though Charitie be now yclad in clay).

Heare Shepheards oft (thereby great wisdome growes),
With good advice a sober answere make:
Be not remoov'd with every winde that blowes,
(That course doo onely sinfull sinners take).   370
Thy talke will shew thy fame or els thy shame;
(A pratling tongue doth often purchase blame).

Obtaine a faithfull frend that will not faile thee,
Thinke on thy Mothers paine in her child-bearing,
Make no debate, least quickly thou bewaile thee,
Visit the sicke with comfortable chearing:
Pittie the prisner, helpe the fatherlesse,
Revenge the Widdowes wrongs in her distresse.

Thinke on thy grave, remember still thy end,
Let not thy winding-sheete be staind with guilt,   380
Trust not a fained reconciled frend,
More than an open foe (that blood hath spilt)
(Who tutcheth pitch, with pitch shalbe defiled),
Be not with wanton companie beguiled.

Take not a flattring woman to thy wife,
A shameles creature, full of wanton words,
(Whose bad, thy good; whose lust will end thy life,
Cutting thy hart with sharpe two edg'ed swords:)
Cast not thy minde on her whose lookes allure,
But she that shines in Truth and Vertue pure.   390

Praise not thy selfe, let other men commend thee,
Beare not a flattring tongue to glaver anie,
Let Parents due correction not offend thee:
Rob not thy neighbor, seeke the love of manie;
Hate not to heare good Counsell given thee,
Lay not thy money unto Usurie.

Restraine thy steps from too much libertie,
Fulfill not th'envious mans malitious minde;
Embrace thy Wife, live not in lecherie;
Content thyselfe with what Fates have assignde: 400

Be rul'd by Reason, Warning dangers save;
True Age is reverend worship to thy grave.

Be patient in extreame Adversitie,
(Man's chiefest credit growes by dooing well,)
Be not high-minded in Prosperitie;
Falshood abhorre, no lying fable tell.
Give not thy selfe to Sloth (the sinke of Shame,
The moath of Time, the enemie to Fame.)

This leare I learned of a Bel-dame Trot,
(When I was yong and wylde as now thou art):   410
But her good counsell I regarded not;
I markt it with my eares, not with my hart:
But now I finde it too-too true (my Sonne)
When my Age-withered Spring is almost done.

Behold my gray head, full of silver haires,
My wrinckled skin, deepe furrowes in my face:
Cares bring Old-Age, Old-Age increaseth cares;
My Time is come, and I have run my Race:
Winter hath snow'd upon my hoarie head,
And with my Winter all my joyes are dead.   420

And thou love-hating Boy, (whom once I loved),
Farewell, a thousand-thousand times farewell;
My Teares the Marble Stones to ruth have moved;
My sad Complaints the babling Ecchoes tell:
And yet thou wouldst take no compassion on mee,
Scorning that crosse which Love hath laid upon mee.

The hardest steele with fier doth mend his misse,
Marble is mollifyde with drops of Raine;
But thou (more hard than Steele or Marble is)
Doost scorne my Teares, and my true love disdaine,   430
Which for thy sake shall everlasting bee,
Wrote in the Annalls of Eternitie.

By this, the Night (with darknes over-spred)
Had drawne the curtaines of her cole-blacke bed;
And *Cynthia* muffling her face with a clowd,
(Lest all the world of her should be too prowd)
Had taken *Conge* of the sable Night,
(That wanting her cannot be halfe so bright;)

When I poore forlorne man and outcast creature
(Despairing of my Love, depisde of Beautie)   440
Grew male-content, scorning his lovely feature,
That had disdaind my ever-zealous dutie:
I hy'd me homeward by the Moone-shine light;
Forswearing Love, and all his fond delight.

Finis.

The Shepherds Content
Or
The happiness of a harmless life.
Written upon Occasion of the former Subject.

Of all the kindes of common Countrey life,
Me thinkes a Shepheards life is most Content;
His State is quiet Peace, devoyd of strife;

His thoughts are pure from all impure intent,
His Pleasures rate sits at an easie rent:
He beares no mallice in his harmles hart,
Malicious meaning hath in him no part.

He is not troubled with th'afflicted minde,
His cares are onely over silly Sheepe;
He is not unto jealozie inclinde,   10
(Thrice happie man) he knowes not how to weepe;
Whil'st I the Treble in deepe sorrowes keepe:
I cannot keepe the Meane; for why (alas)
Griefes have no meane, though I for meane doe passe.

No Briefes nor Semi-Briefes are in my Songs,
Because (alas) my griefe is seldome short;
My Prick-Song's always full of Largues and Longs,
(Because I never can obtaine the Port
Of my desires: Hope is a happie Fort.)
Prick-song (indeed) because it pricks my hart;   20
And Song, because sometimes I ease my smart.

The mightie Monarch of a royall Realme,
Swaying his Scepter with a Princely pompe;
Of his desires cannot so steare the Healme,
But sometime falls into a deadly dumpe,
When as he heares the shrilly-sounding Trumpe
Of forren Enemies, or home-bred Foes;
His minde of griefe, his hart is full of woes.

Or when bad subjects gainst their Soveraigne
(Like hollow harts) unnaturally rebell,   30
How carefull is he to suppresse againe

Their desperate forces, and their powers to quell
With loyall harts, till all againe be well:
When (being subdu'd) his care is rather more
To keepe them under, than it was before.

Thus he never full of sweete Content,
But either this or that his joy debars:
Noble-men gainst Noble-men are bent,
Now Gentlemen and others fall at jarrs:
Thus is his Countrey full of civill warrs;   40
He still in danger sits, still fearing Death:
For Traitors seeke to stop their Princes breath.

The whylst the other hath no enemie,
Without it be the Wolfe, and cruell Fates
(Which no man spare): when as his disagree
He with his sheep-hooke knaps them on the pates,
Schooling his tender Lambs from wanton gates:
Beasts are more kinde then Men, Sheepe seeke not blood
But countrey caytives kill their Countreyes good.

The Courtier he fawn's for his Princes favour,   50
In hope to get a Princely ritch Reward;
His tongue is tipt with honey for to glaver;
Pride deales the Deck whilst Chance doth choose the Card,
Then comes another and his Game hath mard;
Sitting betwixt him, and the morning Sun:
Thus Night is come before the Day is done.

Some Courtiers carefull of their Princes health,
Attend his Person with all dilligence
Whose hand's their hart; whose welfare is their wealth,

Whose safe Protection is their sure Defence,   60
For pure affection, not for hope of pence:
Such is the faithfull hart, such is the minde,
Of him that is to Vertue still inclinde.

The skilfull Scholler, and brave man at Armes,
First plies his Booke, last fights for Countries Peace;
Th'one feares Oblivion, th'other fresh Alarmes:
His paines nere ende, his travailes never cease;
His with the Day, his with the Night increase:
He studies how to get eternall Fame;   70
The Souldier fights to win a glorious Name.

The Knight, the Squire, the Gentleman, the Clowne,
Are full of crosses and calamities;
Lest fickle Fortune should begin to frowne,
And turne their mirth to extreame miseries:
Nothing more certaine than incertainties;
Fortune is full of fresh varietie:
Constant in nothing but inconstancie.

The wealthie Merchant that doth crosse the Seas,
To *Denmarke, Poland, Spaine,* and *Barbarie;*
For all his ritches, lives not still at ease;   80
Sometime he feares ship-spoyling Pyracie,
Another while deceipt and treacherie
Of his owne Factors in a forren Land:
Thus doth he still in dread and danger stand.

Well is he tearmd a Merchant-Venturer,
Since he doth venter lands, and goods, and all:
When he doth travell for his Traffique far,

Little he knowes what fortune may befall,
Or rather what mis-fortune happen shall: 90
Sometimes he splits his Ship against a rocke;
Loosing his men, his goods, his wealth, his stocke.

And if he so escape with life away,
He counts himselfe a man most fortunate,
Because the waves their rigorous rage did stay,
(When being within their cruell powers of late,
The Seas did seeme to pittie his estate)
But yet he never can recover health,
Because his joy was drowned with his wealth.

The painfull Plough-swaine and the Husband-man
Rise up each morning by the breake of day,   100
Taking what toyle and drudging paines they can,
And all is for to get a little stay;
And yet they cannot put their care away:
When Night is come, their cares begin afresh,
Thinking upon their Morrowes busines.

Thus everie man is troubled with unrest,
From rich to poore, from high to low degree:
Therefore I thinke that man is truly blest,
That neither cares for wealth nor povertie,
But laughs at Fortune and her foolerie;   110
That gives rich Churles great store of golde and fee,
And lets poore Schollers live in miserie.

O fading Branches of decaying Bayes
Who now will water your dry-wither'd Armes?
Or where is he that sung the lovely Layes

Of simple Shepheards in their Countrey-Farmes?
Ah he is dead the cause of all our harmes:
And with him dide my joy and sweete delight;
And cleare to Clowdes, the Day is turnd to Night.

SYDNEY, The Syren of this latter Age; 120
SYDNEY, The Blasing-starre of Englands glory;
SYDNEY, The Wonder of the wise and sage;
SYDNEY, The Subject of true Vertues story:
This Syren, Starre, this Wonder, and this Subject;
Is dumbe, dim, gone, and mard by Fortunes Object.

And thou my sweet *Amintas* vertuous minde,
Should I forget thy Learning or thy Love;
Well might I be accounted but unkinde,
Whose pure affection I so oft did prove:
Might my poore Plaints hard stones to pitty move; 130
His losse should be lamented of each Creature,
So great his Name, so gentle was his Nature.

But sleepe his soule in sweet Elysium,
(The happy Haven of eternall rest:)
And let me to my former matter come,
Proving by Reason, Shepheards life is best,
Because he harbours Vertue in his Brest;
And is content (the chiefest thing of all)
With any fortune that shall him befall.

He sits all Day lowd-piping on a Hill, 140
The whilst his flocke about him daunce apace,
His hart with joy, his eares with Musique fill:
Anon a bleating Weather beares the Bace,

A Lambe the Treble; and to his disgrace
Another answers like a middle Meane:
Thus every one to beare a Part are faine.

Like a great King he rules a little Land,
Still making Statutes, and ordayning Lawes,
Which if they breake, he beates them with his Wand:
He doth defend them from the greedy Jawes   150
Of rav'ning Woolves, and Lyons bloudy Pawes.
His Field, his Realme; his Subjects are his Sheepe;
Which he doth still in due obedience keepe.

First he ordaines by Act of Parlament,
(Holden by custome in each Country Towne)
That if a sheepe (with any bad intent)
Presume to breake the neighbour Hedges downe,
Or haunt strange Pastures that be not his owne;
He shall be pounded for his lustines,   160
Untill his Master finde out some redres.

Also if any prove a Strageller
From his owne fellowes in a forraine field,
He shall be taken for a wanderer,
And forc'd himselfe immediatly to yeeld,
Or with a wyde-mouth'd Mastive Curre be kild.
And if not claimd within a twelve-months space,
He shall remaine with Land-lord of the place.

Or if one stray to feede far from the rest,
He shall be pincht by his swift pye-bald Curre;
If any by his fellowes be opprest,   170
The wronger (for he doth all wrong abhorre)

Shall be well bangd so long as he can sturre.

Because he did anoy his harmeles Brother,

That meant not harme to him nor any other.

And last of all, if any wanton Weather,

With briers and brambles teare his fleece in twaine,

He shall be forc'd t'abide cold frosty weather,

And powring showres of ratling stormes of raine,

Till his new fleece begins to grow againe:

And for his rashnes he is doom'd to goe,   180

Without a new Coate all the Winter throw.

Thus doth he keepe them still in awfull feare,

And yet allowes them liberty inough;

So deare to him their welfare doth appeare,

That when their fleeces gin to waxen rough,

He combs and trims them with a Rampicke bough,

Washing them in the streames of silver *Ladon*,

To cleanse their skinnes from all corruption.

Another while he wooes his Country Wench

(With Chaplets crownd, and gaudy girlonds dight)   190

Whose burning Lust her modest eye doth quench,

Standing amazed at her heavenly sight,

(Beauty doth ravish Sense with sweet Delight)

Clearing *Arcadia* with a smoothed Browe

When Sun-bright smiles melts flakes of driven snowe.

Thus doth he frollicke it each day by day,

And when Night comes drawes homeward to his Coate,

Singing a Jigge or merry Roundelay;

(For who sings commonly so merry a Noate,

As he that cannot chop or change a groate.)   200
And in the winter Nights (his chiefe desire)
He turns a Crabbe or Cracknell in the fire.

He leads his Wench a Country Horn-pipe Round,
About a May-pole on a Holy-day;
Kissing his lovely Lasse (with Garlands Crownd)
With whooping heigh-ho singing Care away;
Thus doth he passe the merry month of May:
And all th'yere after in delight and joy,
(Scorning a King) he cares for no annoy.

What though with simple cheere he homely fares?   210
He lives content, a King can doo no more;
Nay not so much, for Kings have manie cares:
But he hath none; except it be that sore
Which yong and old, which vexeth ritch and poore,
The pangs of Love. O! who can vanquish Love,
That conquers Kingdomes, and the Gods above?

Deepe-wounding Arrow, hart-consuming Fire;
Ruler of Reason, slave to tyrant Beautie;
Monarch of harts, Fuell of fond desire,
Prentice to Folly, foe to fained Duetie.   220
Pledge of true Zeale, Affections moitie;
If thou kilst where thou wilt, and whom it list thee,
(Alas) how can a silly Soule resist thee?

By thee great *Collin* lost his libertie,
By thee sweet *Astrophel* forwent his joy.
By thee *Amyntas* wept incessantly,
By thee good *Rowland* liv'd in great annoy;

O cruell, peevish, vylde, blind-seeing Boy:
How canst thou hit their harts, and yet not see?   230
(If thou be blinde, as thou art faind to bee).

A Shepheard loves no ill, but onely thee;
He hath no care, but onely by thy causing:
Why doost thou shoot thy cruell shafts at mee?
Give me some respite, some short time of pausing:
Still my sweet Love with bitter lucke th'art sawcing:
Oh, if thou hast a minde to shew thy might;
Kill mightie Kings, and not a wretched wight.

Yet (O Enthraller of infranchizd harts)
At my poor hart if thou wilt needs be ayming,
Doo me this favour show me both thy Darts,   240
That I may chuse the best for my harts mayming,
(A free consent is privilegd from blaming:)
Then pierce his hard hart with thy golden Arrow,
That thou my wrong, that he may rue my sorrow.

But let mee feele the force of thy lead Pyle,
What should I doo with love when I am old?
I know not how to flatter, fawne, or smyle;
Then stay thy hand, O cruell Bow-man hold:
For if thou strik'st me with thy dart of gold,
I sweare to thee (by *Joves* immortall curse)   250
I have more in my hart, than in my purse.

The more I weepe, the more he bends his Brow,
For in my hart a golden Shaft I finde:
(Cruell, unkinde) and wilt thou leave me so?
Can no remorce nor pittie move thy minde?

Is Mercie in the Heavens so hard to finde?
Oh, then it is no mervaile that on earth,
Of kinde Remorce there is so great a dearth.

How happie were a harmles Shepheards life,
If he had never knowen what Love did meane: 260
But now fond Love in every place is rife,
Staining the purest Soule with spots uncleane,
Making thicke purses, thin; fat bodies, leane:
Love is a fiend, a fire, a heaven, a hell;
Where pleasure, paine, and sad repentence dwell.

There are so manie *Danaes* nowadayes,
That love for lucre; paine for gaine is sold:
No true affection can their fancie please,
Except it be a *Jove* to raine downe gold
Into their laps, which they wyde open hold: 270
If *legem pone* comes, he is receav'd,
When *Vix haud habeo* is of hope bereav'd.

Thus have I showed in my Countrey vaine
The sweet Content that Shepheards still injoy;
The mickle pleasure, and the little paine
That ever doth awayte the Shepheards Boy:
His hart is never troubled with annoy.
He is a King, for he commaunds his Sheepe;
He knowes no woe, for he doth seldome weepe.

He is a Courtier, for he courts his Love;   280
He is a Scholler, for he sings sweet Ditties;
He is a Souldier, for he wounds doth prove;
He is the fame of Townes, the shame of Citties:

He scornes false Fortune, but true Vertue pitties.
He is a Gentleman, because his nature
Is kinde and affable to everie Creature.

Who would not then a simple Shepheard bee,
Rather than be a mightie Monarch made?
Since he injoyes such perfect libertie,
As never can decay, nor never fade: 290
He seldome sits in dolefull Cypresse shade,
But lives in hope, in joy, in peace, in blisse:
Joying all joy with this content of his.

But now good-fortune lands my little Boate
Upon the shoare of his desired rest:
Now must I leave (awhile) my rurall noate,
To thinke on him whom my soule loveth best;
He that can make the most unhappie, blest:
In whose sweete lap Ile lay me downe to sleepe,
And never wake till Marble-stones shall weepe. 300

Finis.

SONNET

Loe here behold these tributerie Teares,
Paid to thy faire, but cruell tyrant Eyes;
Loe here the blossome of my youthfull yeares,
Nipt with the fresh of thy Wraths winter, dyes,

Here on Loves Altar I doo offer up
This burning hart for my Soules sacrifice;
Here I receave this deadly-poysned Cup,
Of *Circe* charm'd; wherein deepe Magicke lyes.

Then Teares (if you be happie Teares indeed),
And Hart (if thou be lodged in his brest),
And Cup (if thou canst helpe despaire with speed);

Teares, Hart, and Cup conjoyne to make me blest:
Teares move, Hart win, Cup cause, ruth, love, desire,
In word, in deed, by moane, by zeale, by fire.

Finis.

The Complaint of Chastitie.

Briefely touching the cause of the death of *Matilda Fitzwalters* an English Ladie; sometime loved of King *John*, after poysoned. The Storie is at large written by *Michael Dreyton*.

You modest Dames, inricht with Chastitie.
Maske your bright eyes with *Vestaes* sable Vaile,
Since few are left so faire or chast as shee;
(Matter for me to weepe, you to bewaile):
For manie seeming so, of Vertue faile;
Whose lovely Cheeks (with rare vermilion tainted)
Can never blush because their faire is painted.

O faire-foule Tincture, staine of Woman-kinde,
Mother of Mischiefe, Daughter of Deceate,
False traitor to the Soule, blot to the Minde,   10
Usurping Tyrant of true Beauties seate,
Right Cousner of the eye, lewd Follies baite,

The flag of filthines, the sinke of shame,
The Divells dye, dishonour of thy name.

Monster of Art, Bastard of bad Desier,
Il-worshipt Idoll, false Imagerie,
Ensigne of Vice, to thine owne selfe a lier,
Silent Inchaunter, mindes Anatomie,
Sly Bawd to Lust, Pandor to Infamie,
Slaunder of Truth, Truth of Dissimulation;   20
Staining our Clymate more than anie Nation.

What shall I say to thee? thou scorne of Nature,
Blacke spot of sinne, vylde lure of lecherie;
Injurious Blame to everie faemale creature,
Wronger of time, Broker of trecherie,
Trap of greene youth, false Womens witcherie,
Hand-maid of pride, high-way to wickednesse;
Yet path-way to Repentance, nerethelesse.

Thou dost entice the minde to dooing evill,
Thou setst dissention twixt the man and wife;   30
A Saint in show, and yet indeed a devill:
Thou art the cause of everie common strife;
Thou art the life of Death, the death of Life;
Thou doost betray thyselfe to Infamie,
When thou art once discerned by the eye.

Ah, little knew *Matilda* of thy being,
Those times were pure from all impure complection;
Then Love came of Desert, Desire of seeing,
Then Vertue was the mother of Affection;
(But Beautie now is under no subjection)   40

Then women were the same that men did deeme,
But now they are the same they doo not seeme.

What faemale now intreated of a King
With gold and jewels, pearles and precious stones,
Would willingly refuse so sweete a thing?
Onely for a little show of Vertue ones?
Women have kindnes grafted in their bones.
Gold is a deepe-perswading Orator,
Especially where few the fault abhor.

But yet shee rather deadly poyson chose,   50
(Oh cruell Bane of most accursed Clime;)
Than staine that milke-white Mayden-virgin Rose,
Which shee had kept unspotted till that time:
And not corrupted with this earthly slime,
Her soule shall live: inclosd eternally,
In that pure shrine of Immortality.

This is my Doome: and this shall come to passe,
For what are Pleasures but still-vading joyes?
Fading as flowers, brittle as a glasse,
Or Potters Clay, crost with the least annoyes;   60
All thinges in this life are but trifling Toyes:
But Fame and Vertue never shall decay,
For Fame is Toomblesse, Vertue lives for aye.

Finis

Hellens Rape
or
A light Lanthorne for light Ladies.
Written in English Hexameters.

Lovely a Lasse, so loved a Lasse, and (alas) such a loving

Lasse, for a while (but a while) was none such a sweet bonny Love-
Lasse

As *Helen, Maenelaus* loving, lov'd, lovelie a love-lasse,

Till spightfull Fortune from a love-lasse made her a love-lesse

Wife. From a wise woman to a witles wanton abandond,

When her mate (unawares) made warres in *Peloponessus,*

Adultrous *Paris* (then a Boy) kept sheepe as a shepheard

On *Ida* Mountaine, unknowne to the King for a Keeper

Of sheep, on *Ida* Mountaine, as a Boy, as a shepheard:

Yet such sheep he kept, and was so seemelie a shepheard,   10

Seemelie a Boy, so seemelie a youth, so seemelie a Younker,

That on *Ide* was not such a Boy, such a youth, such a Younker.

Sonne now reconcil'd to the Father, fained a letter

Sent him by *Jupiter* (the greatest God in *Olympus)*

For to repaire with speede to the bravest Graecian Haven

And to redeeme againe *Hesyone* latelie revolted

From *Troy* by *Ajax,* whom she had newly betrothed.

Well, so well he told his tale to his Aunt *Amaryllis*

That *Amaryllis,* (his Aunt) obtained aid of his aged

Syre, that he sent him a ship, and made Capten of *Argus.*   20

Great store went to Greece with lust-bewitched *Alexis,*

Telamour, and *Tydias:* with these he sliceth the salt seas,

The salt seas slicing, at length he comes to the firme land,

Firme land an auntient Iland cald old *Lacedaemon.*

Argus (eyefull Earle) when first the ken of a Castle

He had spide bespake: (to the Mate, to the men, to the Mates-man)

Lo behold of Greece (quoth he) the great *Cytadella,*

(Ycleaped *Menela)* so tearmd of *Deliaes* Husband:

Happie *Helen,* Womens most woonder, beautifull *Helen.*

Oh would God (quoth he) with a flattring Tongue he repeated: 30

Oh would God (quoth he) that I might deserve to be husband

To such a happie huswife, to such a beautifull *Helen.*

This he spake to intice the minde of a lecherous young-man:

But what spurres need now, for an untam'd Titt to be trotting:

Or to add old Oile to the flame, new flaxe to the fier:

Paris heard him hard, and gave good eare to his hearkening:

And then his love to a lust, his lust was turnd to a fier,

Fier was turned to a flame, and flame was turnd to a burning

Brand: and mothers Dreame was then most truelie resolved.

Well so far th'are come, that now thare come to the Castle,   40

Castle all of stone, yet every stone was a Castle:

Everie foote had a Fort, and everie Fort had a fountaine,

Everie fountaine a spring, and everie spring had a spurting

Streame: so strong without, within, so stately a building,

Never afore was seene: If never before *Polyphoebe*

Was seene: was to be seene, if nere to be seene was *Olympus.*

Flowers were framed of flints, Walls Rubies, Rafters of Argent:

Pavements of Chrisolite, Windows contriv'd of a Christall:

Vessels were of gold, with gold was each thing adorned:

Golden Webs more worth than a wealthy *Souldan* of Egypt,   50

And her selfe more worth than a wealthy *Souldan* of Egypt:

And her selfe more worth than all the wealth shee possessed;

Selfe? indeede such a selfe, as thundring *Jove* in *Olympus,*

Though he were father could finde in his hart to be husband.

Embassage ended, to the Queene of faire *Lacedaemon;*

(Happie King of a Queene so faire, of a Countrey so famous)

Embassage ended, a Banquet brave was appointed:

Sweet Repast for a Prince, fine Junkets fit for a Kings sonne.

Biskets and Carawayes, Comfets, Tart, Plate, Jelly, Ginge-bread,

Lymons and Medlars: and Dishes moe by a thousand.   60

First they fell to the feast, and after fall to a Dauncing,

And from a Dance to a Trance, from a Trance they fell to a falling,

Either in other armes, and either in armes of another.

Pastime over-past, and Banquet duely prepared,

Devoutly pared: Each one hies home to his owne home,

Save Lord and Ladie: Young Lad, but yet such an old Lad,

In such a Ladies lappe, at such a slipperie by-blow,

That in a world so wide, could not be found such a wilie

Lad: in an Age so old, could not be found such an old lad:

Old lad, and bold lad, such a Boy, such a lustie *Juventus.*   70

Well to their worke they goe, and both they jumble in one Bed:

Worke so well they like, that they still like to be working:

For *Aurora* mounts before he leaves to be mounting:

And *Astraea* fades before she faints to be falling:

(*Helen* a light Huswife, now a lightsome starre in *Olympus.*)

Finis

Cynthia

With Certaine Sonnets,
And the Legend of Cassandra.

Quod cupio nequeo.

At London,
Printed for Humfrey
Lownes, and are to bee
sold at the West doore
of Paules.
1595

To the Right Honorable, and
Most noble-minded Lorde,
William Stanley, Earle of
Darby, &c.

Right Honorable, the dutifull affection I beare to your manie vertues, is cause, that to manifest my love to your Lordship, I am constrained to shew my simplenes to the world. Many are they that admire your worth, of the which number, I (though the meanest in abilitie, yet with the formost in affection) am one that most desire to serve, and onely to serve your Honour.

Small is the gift, but great is my good-will; the which, by how much the lesse I am able to express it, by so much the more it is infinite. Live long: and inherit your Predecessors vertues, as you doe their dignitie and estate. This is my wish: the which your honorable excellent giftes doe promise me to obtaine: and whereof these few rude and unpollished lines, are a true (though an undeserving) testimony. If my ability were better, the signes should be greater; but being as it is, your honour must take me as I am, not as I should be. My yeares being so young, my perfection cannot be great: But howsoever it is, yours it is; and I myselfe am yours; in all humble service, most ready to be commaunded.

Richard Barnefeilde.

To the curteous Gentlemen Readers.

Gentlemen: the last Terme there came forth a little toy of mine, intituled, *The affectionate Shepheard:* In the which, his Country *Content* found such friendly favor, that it hath incouraged me to publish my second fruites. *The affectionate Shepheard* being the first: howsoever undeservedly (I protest) I have beene thought (of some) to have beene the authour of two Books heretofore. I neede not to name them, because they are two-well knowne already: nor will I deny them, because they are dislik't; but because they are not mine. This protestation (I hope) will satisfie th'indifferent: as for them that are maliciously envious, as I cannot, so I care not to please. Some there were, that did interpret *The affectionate Shepheard,* otherwise then (in truth) I meant, touching the subject thereof, to wit, the love of a Shepheard to a boy; a fault, the which I will not excuse, because I never made. Onely this, I will unshaddow my conceit: being nothing else, but an imitation of *Virgill,* in the second Eglogue of *Alexis.* In one or two places (in this Booke) I use the name of *Eliza* pastorally: wherein, lest any one should misconster my meaning (as I hope none will) I have here briefly discovered my harmeles conceipt as concerning that name: whereof once (in a simple Shepheards device) I wrot this Epigramme.

To this for beautie; fairest on the earth.

Thus, hoping you will beare with my rude conceit of *Cynthia,* (if for no other cause, yet, for that it is the first imitation of the verse of that excellent Poet, Maister *Spencer,* in his *Fayrie Queene)* I leave you to the reading of that, which I so much desire may breed your Delight.

Richard Barnefeild.

T.T. in commendation of the Authour his worke.

Whylom that in a shepheards gray coate masked,
(Where masked love the nonage of his skill)
Reares new Eagle-winged pen, new tasked,
To scale the by-clift Muse sole-pleasing hill:
Dropping sweete Nectar poesie from his quill,
Admires faire CYNTHIA with his ivory pen
Faire CHYTHIA lov'd, fear'd, of Gods and men.

Downe sliding from that cloudes ore-pearing mounteine:
Decking with double grace the neighbour plaines,

Drawes christall dew, from PEGASE foote-sprung fountain,
Whose flower set banks, delights, sweet choice containes:
Nere yet discoverd to the country swaines:
Heere bud those branches, which adorne his turtle,
With love made garlands, of heart-bleeding Mirtle.

Rays'd from the cynders, of the thrice-sact towne:
ILLIONS sooth-telling SYBILLIST appeares,
Eclipsing PHOEBUS love, with scornefull frowne,
Whose tragicke end, affords warme-water teares,
(For pitty-wanting PACOE, none forbeares)
Such period haps, to beauties price ore-priz'd:
Where JANUS-faced love, doth lurke disguiz'd.

Nere-waining CYNTHIA yeelds thee triple thankes,
Whose beames unborrowed darke the worlds faire eie,
And as full streames that ever fill their bankes,
So those rare Sonnets, where wits ripe doth lie,
With Trojan Nimph, doe soare thy fame to skie,
And those, and these, contend thy Muse to raise
(Larke mounting Muse) with more then common praise.

To His Mistress

Bright Starre of Beauty, fairest Faire alive,
Rare president of peerelesse chastity;
(In whom the Muses and the Graces strive,
Which shall possesse the chiefest part of thee:)
Oh let these simple lines accepted bee:
Which here I offer at thy sacred shrine:
Sacred, because sweet Beauty is divine.

And though I cannot please each curious eare,
With sugred Noates of heavenly Harmonie:

Yet if my love shall to thy selfe appeare,
No other Muse I will invoke but thee:
And if thou wilt my faire *Thalia* be,
Ile sing sweet Hymnes and praises to thy name,
In that cleare Temple of eternall Fame.

But ah (alas) how can mine infant Muse
(That never heard of *Helicon* before)
Performe my promise past: when they refuse
Poore Shepheards Plaints? yet will I still adore
Thy sacred Name, although I write no more:
Yet hope I shall, if this accepted bee:
If not, in silence sleepe eternally.

Cynthia

Now was the Welkyn all invelloped
With duskie Mantle of the sable Night:
And CYNTHIA lifting up her drouping head,
Blusht at the Beautie of her borrowed light,
When Sleepe now summon'd every mortal wight.
Then loe (me thought) I saw or seem'd to see,
An heavenly Creature like an Angell bright,
That in great heaste came pacing towards me:
Was never mortall eye beheld so faire a Shee.

Thou lazie man (quoth she) what mak'st thou here   10
(Luld in the lap of Honours Enimie?)
I heere commaund thee now for to appeare
(By vertue of JOVES mickle Majestie)
In yonder Wood. (Which with her finger shee
Out-poynting) had no sooner turn'd her face,
And leaving mee to muze what she should bee,

Yvanished into some other place:
But straite (me thought) I saw a rout of heavenlie Race.

Downe in a Dale, hard by a Forrest side,
(Under the shaddow of a loftie Pine,)   20
Not far from whence a trickling streame did glide,
Did nature by her secret art combine,
A pleasant Arbour, of a spreading Vine:
Wherein Art stove with nature to compaire,
That made it rather seeme a thing divine,
Being scituate all in the open Aire:
A fairer neer was seene, if any seene so faire.

There might one see, and yet not see (indeede)
Fresh *Flora* flourishing in chiefest Prime;
Arrayed all in gay and gorgeous weede,   30
The Primrose and sweet-smelling Eglantine,
As fitted best beguiling so the time:
And ever as she went she strewd the place,
Red-roses mixt with Daffadillies fine,
For Gods and Goddesses, that in like case
In this same order sat, with il-beseeming grace.

First, in a royall Chaire of massie gold,
(Bard all about with plates of burning steele)
Sat *Jupiter* most glorious to behold,
And in his hand was placed Fortunes wheele: 40
The which he often turn'd, and oft did reele.
And next to him, in griefe and gealouzie,
(If sight may censure what the heart doth feele)
In sad lament was placed *Mercurie;*
That dying seem'd to weep, and weeping seem'd to die.

On th'other side, above the other twaine,
(Delighting as it seem'd to sit alone)

Sat *Mulciber;* in pride and high disdaine,
Mounted on high upon a stately throne,
And even with that I heard a deadly grone: 50
Muzing at this, and such an uncouth sight,
(Not knowing what shoulde make that piteous mone)
I saw three furies, all in Armour dight,
With every one a Lampe, and every one a light.

I deemed so; nor was I much deceav'd,
For poured forth in sensuall Delight,
There might I see of Sences quite bereav'd
King *Priams* Sonne, that *Alexander* hight
(Wrapt in the Mantle of eternall Night.)
And under him, awaiting for his fall, 60
Sate Shame, here Death, and there sat fel Despight,
That with their Horrour did his heart appall:
Thus was his Blisse to Bale, his Hony turn'd to gall.

In which delight feeding mine hungry eye,
Of two great Goddesses a sight I had,
And after them in wondrous Jollity,
(As one that inly joyd, so was she glad)
The Queene of Love full royallie yclad,
In glistring Gold, and peerelesse precious stone,
There might I spie: and her Companion bad, 70
Proud *Paris,* Nephew to *Laomedon,*
That afterward did cause the Death of many a one.

By this the formost melting all in teares,
And rayning downe resolved Pearls in showers,
Gan to approach the place of heavenly Pheares,
And with her weeping, watring all their Bowers,
Throwing sweet Odors on those fading flowers,
At length, she them bespake thus mournfullie.

High *Jove* (quoth she) and yee Coelestiall powers,
That here in Judgement sit twixt her and mee,   80
Now listen (for a while) and judge with equitie.

Sporting our selves to day, as wee were woont,
(I meane, I, *Pallas,* and the Queene of Love,
Intending with *Diana* for to hunt,
On *Ida* Mountaine top our skill to prove,
A golden Ball was trindled from above,
And on the Rinde was writ this Poesie,
PULCHERIMAE for which a while we strove,
Each saying shee was fairest of the three,
When loe a shepheards Swaine not far away we see.   90

I spi'd him first, and spying thus bespake,
Shall yonder swaine unfolde the mysterie?
Agreed (quoth *Venus)* and by *Stygian* Lake,
To whom he gives the ball so shall it bee:
Nor from his censure will I flie, quoth shee,
(Poynting to *Pallas)* though I loose the gole.
Thus every one yplac'd in her degree,
The Shepheard comes, whose partiall eies gan role,
And on our beuties look't, and of our beuties stole.

I promis'd wealth, *Minerva* promised wit,   100
(Shee promis'd wit to him that was unwise,)
But he (fond foole) had soone refused it,
And minding to bestow that glorious Prize,
On *Venus,* that with pleasure might suffize
His greedie minde in loose lasciviousnes:
Upon a sudden, wanting goode advice,
Holde heere (quoth he) this golden Ball possesse,
Which *Paris* gives to thee for meede of worthines,

Thus have I shew'd the summe of all my sute,
And as a Plaintiffe heere appeale to thee,   110
And to the rest. Whose folly I impute
To filthie lust, and partialitie,
That made him judge amisse: and so doo we
(Quoth *Pallas, Venus),* nor will I gaine-say,
Although it's mine by right, yet willinglie,
I heere disclaime my title and obey:
When silence being made, *Jove* thus began to saie.

Thou *Venus,* art my darling, thou my deare,
(Minerva,) shee, my sister and my wife:
So that of all a due respect I beare,   120
Assign'd as one to end this doubtfull strife,
(Touching your forme, your fame, your love, your life)
Beauty is vaine much like a gloomy light,
And wanting wit is counted but a trife,
Especially when Honour's put to flight:
Thus of a lovely, soone becomes a loathly sight.

Wit without wealth is bad, yet counted good,
Wealth wanting wisdom's worse, yet deem'd as wel,
From whence (for ay) doth flow, as from a flood,
A pleasant Poyson, and a heavenly Hell,   130
Where mortall men do covet still to dwell.
Yet one there is to Vertue so inclin'd,
That as for Majesty she beares the Bell,
So in the truth who tries her princelie minde,
Both Wisdom, Beauty, Wealth, and all in her shall find.

In Westerne world amids the Ocean maine,
In compleat Vertue shining like the Sunne,
In great Renowne a maiden Queene doth raigne,
Whose royall Race, in Ruine first begun,

Till Heavens bright Lamps dissolve shall nere be done: 140
In whose faire eies Love linckt with vertues been,
In everlasting Peace and Union.
Which sweet Consort in her full well beseeme
Of Bounty, and of Beauty fairest Fayrie Queene.

And to conclude, the gifts in her yfound,
Are all so noble, royall, and so rare,
That more and more in her they doe abound;
In her most peerelesse Prince without compare,
Endowing still her minde with vertuous care:
That through the world (so wide) the flying fame,   150
(And Name that Envies selfe cannot impaire),
Is blown of this faire Queen, this gorgeous dame,
Fame borrowing al men's mouths to royalize the same.

And with this sentence *Jupiter* did end,
This is the Pricke (quoth he), this is the praies,
To whom, this as a Present I will send,
That shameth *Cynthia* in her silver Raies,
If so you three this deed doe not displease.
Then one, and all, and every one of them,
To her that is the honour of her daies,   160
A second *Judith* in JERUSALEM,
To her we send this Pearle, this Jewell, and this Jem.

Then call'd he up the winged *Mercury,*
(The mighty Messenger of Gods enrold)
And bad him hither hastily to hie,
Whom tended by her Nymphes he should behold,
(Like Pearles ycouched all in shining gold.)
And even with that, from pleasant slumbring sleepe,
(Desiring much these wonders to unfold)

I wak'ning, when *Aurora* gan to peepe,   170
Depriv'd so soone of my sweet Dreame, gan almost weepe.

The Conclusion

Thus, sacred Virgin, Muse of chastitie,
This difference is betwixt the Moone and thee:
Shee shines by Night; but thou by Day do'st shine:
Shee Monthly changeth; thou dost nere decline:
And as the Sunne, to her, doth lend his light,
So hee, by thee, is onely made so bright:
Yet neither Sun, nor Moone, thou canst be named,
Because thy light hath both their beauties shamed:
Then, since an heavenly Name doth thee befall,   180
Thou VIRGO art: (if any Signe at all).

Finis.

SONNET I

Sporting at fancie, setting light by love,
There came a theefe and stole away my heart,
(And therefore robd me of my chiefest part)
Yet cannot Reason him a felon prove.
For why his beauty (my hearts theefe) affirmeth,
Piercing no skin (the bodies fensive wall)
And having leave, and free consent withall,
Himselfe not guilty, from love guilty tearmeth,
Conscience the Judge, twelve Reasons are the Jurie,
They finde mine eies the beutie t'have let in,
And on this verdict given, agreed they bin,

Wherefore, because his beauty did allure yee,
Your Doome is this: in teares still to be drowned,
When his faire forehead with disdain is frowned.

SONNET II

Beuty and Majesty are falne at ods,
Th'one claimes his cheeke, the other claimes his chin;
Then Vertue comes, and puts her title in.
(Quoth she) I make him like th'immortall Gods.
(Quoth Majestie) I owne his lookes, his Brow,
His lips, (quoth Love) his eies, his faire is mine.
And yet (quoth Majesty) he is not thine,
I mixe Disdaine with Loves congealed Snow.
I, but (quoth Love) his lockes are mine (by right)
His stately gate is mine (quoth Majestie,)
And mine (quoth Vertue) is his Modestie.
Thus as they strive about this heavenly wight,
At last the other two to Vertue yeeld,
The lists of Love, fought in faire Beauties field.

SONNET III

The Stoicks thinke, (and they come neere the truth,)
That vertue is the chiefest good of all,
The Academicks on *Idea* call.
The Epicures in pleasure spend their youth,
The Perrepatetickes judge felicitie,
To be the chiefest good above all other,
One man, thinks this: and that conceaves another:
So that in one thing very few agree.
Let Stoicks have their Vertue if they will,
And all the rest their chiefe-supposed good,

Let cruell Martialists delight in blood,
And Mysers joy their bags with gold to fill:
My chiefest good, my chiefe felicity,
Is to be gazing on my loves faire eie.

SONNET IIII

Two stars there are in one faire firmament,
(Of some intitled *Ganymedes* sweet face),
Which other stars in brightnes doe disgrace,
As much as *Po* in clearnes passeth *Trent.*
Nor are they common natur'd stars: for why,
These stars when other shine vaile their pure light,
And when all other vanish out of sight,
They adde a glory to the worlds great eie.
By these two stars my life is onely led,
In them I place my joy, in them my pleasure,
Love's piercing Darts, and Natures precious treasure
With their sweet foode my fainting soule is fed:
Then when my sunne is absent from my sight
How can it chuse (with me) but be dark night?

SONNET V

It is reported of faire *Thetis* Sonne,
(*Achilles* famous for his chivalry,
His noble minde and magnanimity,)
That when the Trojan wars were new begun,
Whos'ever was deepe-wounded with his speare,
Could never be recured of his maime,
Nor ever after be made whole againe:
Except with that speares rust he holpen were.
Even so it fareth with my fortune now,

Who being wounded with his piercing eie,
Must either thereby finde a remedy,
Or els to be releev'd, I know not how,
Then if thou hast a minde still to annoy me,
Kill me with kisses, if thou wilt destroy me.

SONNET VI

Sweet Corrall lips, where Nature's treasure lies,
The balme of blisse, the soveraigne salve of sorrow,
The secret touch of loves heart-burning arrow,
Come quench my thirst or els poor *Daphnis* dies.
One night I dreamd (alas twas but a Dreame)
That I did feele the sweetnes of the same,
Where-with inspir'd, I young againe became,
And from my heart a spring of blood did streame,
But when I wak't, I found it nothing so,
Save that my limbs (me thought) did waxe more strong
And I more lusty far, and far more yong.
This gift on him rich Nature did bestow.
Then if in dreaming so, I so did speede,
What should I doe, if I did so indeede?

SONNET VII

Sweet *Thames* I honour thee, not for thou art
The chiefest River of the fairest Ile,
Nor for thou dost admirers eies beguile,
But for thou hold'st the keeper of my heart,
For on thy waves, (thy Christal-billow'd waves)
My fairest faire, my silver Swan is swimming:
Against the sunne his pruned feathers trimming:
Whilst *Neptune* his faire feete with water laves,

Neptune, I feare not thee, not yet thine eie,
And yet (alas) *Apollo* lov'd a boy,
And *Cyparissus* was *Silvanus* joy.
No, no, I feare none but faire *Thetis*, I,
For if she spie my Love, (alas) aie me,
My mirth is turn'd to extreame miserie.

SONNET VIII

Sometimes I wish that I his pillow were,
So might I steale a kisse, and yet not seene,
So might I gaze upon his sleeping eine,
Although I did it with a panting feare:
But when I well consider how vaine my wish is,
Ah foolish bees (thinke I) that doe not sucke
His lips for hony; but poore flowers doe plucke
Which have no sweet in them: when his sole kisses,
Are able to revive a dying soule.
Kisse him, but sting him not, for if you doe,
His angry voice your flying will pursue:
But when they heare his tongue, what can controule,
Their back-returne? for then they plaine may see,
How hony-combs from his lips dropping bee.

SONNET IX

Diana (on a time) walking the wood,
To sport herselfe, of her faire traine forlorne,
Chaunc't for to pricke her foote against a thorne,
And from thence issu'd out a streame of blood.
No sooner shee was vanisht out of sight,
But loves faire Queen came there away by chance,
And having of this hap a glym'ring glance,

She put the blood into a christall bright,
When being now come unto mount *Rhodope,*
With her faire hands she formes a shape of Snow,
And blends it with this blood; from whence doth grow
A lovely creature, brighter than the Dey.
And being christned in faire *Paphos* shrine,
She call'd him *Ganymede:* as all divine.

SONNET X

Thus was my love, thus was my *Ganymed,*
(Heavens joy, worlds wonder, natures fairest work,
In whose aspect Hope and Dispaire doe lurke)
Made of pure blood in whitest snow yshed,
And for sweete *Venus* only form'd his face,
And his each member delicately framed,
And last of all faire *Ganymede* him named,
His limbs (as their Creatrix) her imbrace.
But as for his pure, spotles, vertuous minde,
Because it sprung of chaste *Dianaes* blood,
(Goddess of Maides, directresse of all good,)
Hit wholy is to chastity inclinde.
And thus it is: as far as I can prove,
He loves to be belov'd, but not to love.

SONNET XI

Sighing, and sadly sitting by my Love,
He ask't the cause of my hearts sorrowing,
Conjuring me by heavens eternall King
To tell the cause which me so much did move.
Compell'd: (quoth I) to thee will I confesse,
Love is the cause; and only love it is

That doth deprive me of my heavenly blisse.
Love is the paine that doth my heart oppresse.
And what is she (quoth he) whom thou do'st love?
Looke in this glasse (quoth I) there shalt thou see
The perfect forme of my faelicitie.
When, thinking that it would strange Magique prove,
He open'd it: and taking off the cover,
He straight perceav'd himselfe to be my Lover.

SONNET XII

Some talke of *Ganymede* th'*Idalian* Boy,
And some of faire *Adonis* make their boast,
Some talke of him whom lovely *Laeda* lost,
And some of *Ecchoes* love that was so coy.
They speake by heere-say, I of perfect truth,
They partially commend the persons named,
And for them, sweet Encomions have framed:
I onely t'him have sacrifiz'd my youth.
As for those wonders of antiquitie,
And those whom later ages have injoy'd,
(But ah what hath not cruell death destroide?
Death, that envies this worlds felicitie),
They were (perhaps) lesse faire then Poets write.
But he is fairer then I can indite.

SONNET XIII

Speake Eccho, tell; how may I call my love?   *Love.*
But how his Lamps that are so christaline?   *Eyne.*
Oh happy starrs that make your heavens divine:
And happy Jems that admiration move.
How tearm'st his golden tresses wav'd with aire?   *Haire.*

Oh lovely haire of your more-lovely Maister,
Image of love, faire shape of Alablaster,
Why do'st thou drive thy Lover to dispaire?
How do'st thou cal the bed wher beuty grows?   *Rose.*
Faire virgine-Rose, whose mayden blossoms cover
The milke-white Lilly, thy imbracing Lover:
Whose kisses makes thee oft thy red to love.
And blushing oft for shame, when he hath kist thee,
He vades away, and thou raing'st where it list thee.

SONNET XIIII

Here: hold this glove (this milk-white cheveril glove)
Not quaintly over-wrought with curious knots,
Not deckt with golden spangs, nor silver spots,
Yet wholsome for thy hand as thou shalt prove.
Ah no: (sweet boy) place this glove neere thy heart,
Weare it, and lodge it still within thy brest,
So shalt thou make me (most unhappy,) blest.
So shalt thou rid my paine, and ease my smart:
How can that be (perhaps) thou wilt reply,
A glove is for the hand not for the heart,
Nor can it well be prov'd by common art,
Nor reasons rule. To this, thus answere I:
If thou from glove do'st take away the g,
Then glove is love: and so I send it thee.

SONNET XV

Ah fairest *Ganymede*, disdaine me not,
Though silly Sheepeheard I, presume to love thee,
Though my harsh songs and Sonnets cannot move thee,
Yet to thy beauty is my love no blot.

Apollo, Jove, and many Gods beside,
S'daind not the name of cuntry shepheards swains,
Nor want we pleasure, though we take some pains,
We live contentedly: a thing call'd pride,
Which so corrupts the Court and every place,
(Each place I meane where learning is neglected,
And yet of late, even learnings selfe's infected)
I know not what it meanes, in any case:
Wee onely (when *Molorchus* gins to peepe)
Learne for to folde, and to unfold our sheepe.

SONNET XVI

Long have I long'd to see my Love againe,
Still have I wisht, but never could obtaine it;
Rather than all the world (if I might gaine it)
Would I desire my loves sweet precious gaine.
Yet in my soule I see him everie day,
See him, and see his still sterne countenaunce,
But (ah) what is of long continuance,
Where Majestie and Beautie beares the sway?
Sometimes, when I imagine that I see him,
(As love is full of foolish fantasies)
Weening to kisse his lips, as my loves fee's,
I feele but Aire: nothing but Aire to bee him.
Thus with *Ixion,* kisse I clouds in vaine:
Thus with *Ixion,* feele I endles paine.

SONNET XVII

Cherry-lipt *Adonis* in his snowie shape,
Might not compare with his pure Ivorie white,
On whose faire front a Poets pen may write,

Whose rosiate red excels the crimson grape,
His love-enticing delicate soft limbs,
Are rarely fram'd t'intrap poore gazing eies:
His cheekes, the Lillie and Carnation dies,
With lovely tincture which *Apolloes* dims.
His lips ripe strawberries in Nectar wet,
His mouth a Hive, his tongue a hony-combe,
Where Muses (like Bees) make their mansion.
His teeth pure Pearle in blushing Correll set.
Oh how can such a body sinne-procuring,
Be slow to love, and quicke to hate, enduring?

SONNET XVIII

Not *Megaboetes* nor *Cleonymus,*
(Of whom great *Plutarck* makes such mention,
Praysing their faire with rare invention)
As *Ganymede* were halfe so beauteous.
They onely pleas'd the eies of two great Kings,
But all the worlde at my love stands amazed,
Nor one that on his Angels face hath gazed,
But (ravisht with delight) him Presents brings.
Some weaning Lambs, and some a suckling Kyd,
Some Nuts, and fil-beards, others Peares and Plums,
Another with a milk-white Heyfar comes;
As lately *Aegons* man *(Damoetas)* did:
But neither he, nor all the Nymphs beside,
Can win my *Ganymede;* with them t'abide.

SONNET XIX

Ah no; nor I my selfe: though my pure love
(Sweete *Ganymede)* to thee hath still beene pure,

And even till my last gaspe shall aie endure,
Could ever thy obdurate beuty move:
Then cease oh'Goddesse sonne (for sure thou art,
A Goddesse sonne that canst resist desire)
Cease thy hard heart, and entertaine loves fire,
Within thy sacred breast: by Natures art.
And as I love thee more than any Creature,
(Love thee, because thy beautie is divine;
Love thee, because my selfe, my soule is thine:
Wholie devoted to thy lovelie feature)
Even so of all the vowels, I and U,
Are dearest unto me, as doth ensue.

SONNET XX

But now my Muse toyld with continuall care,
Begins to faint, and slacke her former pace,
Expecting favour from that heavenly grace,
That maie (in time) her feeble strength repaire.
Till when (sweete youth) th'essence of my soule,
(Thou that dost sit and sing at my hearts griefe.
Thou that dost send thy shepheard no reliefe)
Beholde, these lines; the sonnes of Teares and Dole.
Ah had great *Colin* chiefe of shepheards all,
Or gentle *Rowland,* my professed friend,
Had they thy beautie, or my pennance pend,
Greater had beene thy fame, and lesse my fall:
But since that everie one cannot be wittie,
Pardon I crave of them, and of thee, pitty.

Finis.

An Ode

Nights were short, and daies were long;
Blossoms on the Hauthorn's hung:
Philomoele (Night-Musiques-King)
Tolde the comming of the spring.
Whose sweete silver-sounding voice
Made the little birds rejoice:
Skipping light from spray to spray,
Till *Aurora* shewd the day.
Scarce might one see, when I might see
(For such chaunces sudden bee)   10
By a well of Marble-stone
A Shepheard lying all alone.
Weepe he did; and his weeping
Made the fading flowers spring.
Daphnis was his name (I weene)
Youngest Swaine of Summers Queene.
When *Aurora* saw 'twas he.
Weepe she did for companie:
Weepe she did for her sweete sonne
That (when antique *Troy* was wonne)   20
Suffer'd death by lucklesse fate,
Whom she now laments too late:
And each morning (by Cocks crew)
Showers downe her silver dew.
Whose teares (falling from their spring)
Give moysture to each living thing,
That on earth increase and grow,
Through power of their friendlie foe.

Whose effect when *Flora* felt,

Teares, that did her bosome melt,   30

(For who can resist teares often,

But Shee whom no teares can soften?)

Peering straite above the banks,

Shew'd herselfe to give her thanks.

Wondring thus at Natures worke,

(Wherein many marvailes lurke)

Me thought I heard a dolefull noise,

Consorted with a mournfull voice,

Drawing nie to heare more plaine,

Heare I did, unto my paine,   40

(For who is not pain'd to heare

Him in griefe whom heart holdes deare?)

Silly swaine (with griefe ore-gone)

Thus to make his piteous mone.

Love I did, (alas the while)

Love I did, but did beguile

My deare love with loving so,

(Whom as then I did not know.)

Love I did the fairest boy,

That these fields did ere enjoy.   50

Love I did, fair *Ganymed;*

(Venus darling, beauties bed:)

Him I thought the fairest creature,

Him the quintessence of Nature:

But yet (alas) I was deceiv'd,

(Love of reason is bereav'd)

For since then I saw a Lasse

(Lasse) that did in beauty passe,

(Passe) faire *Ganymede* as farre
As *Phoebus* doth the smallest starre.   60
Love commaunded me to love;
Fancy bade me not remove
My affection from the swaine
Whom I never could obtaine:
(For who can obtaine that favour,
Which he cannot graunt the craver?)
Love at last (though loath) prevailde;
(Love) that so my heart assailde;
Wounding me with her faire eies,
(Ah how Love can subtelize,   70
And devize a thousand shifts,
How to worke men to his drifts.)
Her it is, for whom I mourne;
Her, for whom my life I scorne;
Her, for whom I weepe all day;
Her, for whom I sigh, and say,
Either She, or else no creature,
Shall enjoy my love: whose feature
Though I never can obtaine,
Yet shall my true love remaine: 80
Till (my body turn'd to clay)
My poore soule must passe away,
To the heavens; where (I hope)
Hit shall finde a resting scope:
Then since I loved thee (alone)
Remember me when I am gone.
Scarce had he these last words spoken,
But me thought his heart was broken;

With great griefe that did abound,
(Cares and griefe the heart confound)   90
In whose heart (thus riv'd in three)
ELIZA written I might see:
In Caracters of crimson blood,
(Whose meaning well I understood.)
Which, for my heart might not behold,
I hyed me home my sheep to folde.

Finis.

Cassandra

Upon a gorgious gold embossed bed,
With Tissue curtaines drawne against the sunne,
(Which gaizers eies into amazement led,
So curiously the workmanship was done,)
Lay faire *Cassandra*, in her snowie smocke,
Whose lips the Rubies and the pearles did locke.

And from her Ivory front hung dangling downe,
A bush of long and lovely curled haire;
Whose head impalled with a precious Crowne
Of orient Pearle, made her to seeme more faire: 10
And yet more faire she hardly could be thought,
Then Love and Nature in her face had wrought.

By this young *Phoebus* rising from the East,
Had tane a view of this rare Paragon:
Wherewith he soone his radiant beames addresst,
And with great joy her (sleeping) gazed upon:

Til at the last, through her light casements cleare,
He stole a kisse: and softly call'd her Deare.

Yet not so softly but (therwith awak't,)
Shee gins to open her faire christall covers,   20
Wherewith the wounded God, for terror quakt,
(Viewing those darts that kill disdained lovers:)
And blushing red to see himselfe so shamed
He scorns his Coach, and his owne beauty blamed.

Now with a trice he leaves the azure skies,
(As whilome *Jove* did at *Europaes* rape,)
And ravisht with her love-aluring eies,
He turns himselfe into a humane shape:
And that his wish the sooner might ensue,
He sutes himselfe like one of *Venus* crew.   30

Upon his head he wore a Hunters hat
Of crimson velvet, spangd with stars of gold,
Which grac'd his lovely face: and over that
A silver hatband ritchly to behold:
On his left shoulder hung a loose Tyara,
As whilome us'd faire *Penthesilea*.

Faire *Penthesilea* th'*Amazonian* Queene,
When she to Troy came with her warlike band,
Of brave Viragoes glorious to be seene;
Whose manlike force no power might withstand: 40
So look't *Apollo* in his lovely weedes,
As he unto the Trojan Damzell speedes.

Not faire *Adonis* in his chiefest pride,
Did seeme more faire, then young *Apollo* seemed,
When he through th'aire invisibly did glide,
T'obtaine his Love, which he Angelike deemed:
Whom finding in her chamber all alone,
He thus begins t'expresse his piteous mone.

O fairest, faire, above all faires (quoth hee,)
If ever Love obtained Ladies favour,   50
Then shew thy selfe compassionate to me,
Whose heart surpriz'd with thy divine behaviour,
Yeelds my selfe captive to thy conqu'ring eies:
O then shew mercy, do not tyrannize.

Scarce had *Apollo* utter'd these last words,
(Rayning downe pearle from his immortall eies,)
When she for answere, naught but feare affords,
Filling the place with lamentable cries:
But *Phoebus* fearing much these raging fits,
With sugred kisses sweetely charm'd her lips.   60

(And tells her softly in her softer eare)
That he a God is, and no mortall creature:
Wherewith abandoning all needlesse feare,
(A common frailtie of weake womans nature)
She boldly askes him of his deitie,
Gracing her question with her wanton eie.

Which charge to him no sooner was assignde,
But taking faire *Cassandra* by the hand
(The true bewraier of his secrete minde)
He first begins to let her understand,   70

That he from *Demogorgon* was descended:
Father of th'Earth, of Gods and men commended.

The tenor of which tale he now recites,
Closing each period with a ravisht kisse:
Which kindnes, she unwillingly requites,
Conjoyning oft her Corrall lips to his:
Not that she lov'd the love of any one;
But that she meant to cozen him anone.

Hee briefly t'her relates his pedegree:
The sonne of *Jove*, sole guider of the sunne,   80
He that slue *Python* so victoriouslie,
He that the name of wisdomes God hath wonne,
The God of Musique, and of Poetry:
Of Phisicke, Learning, and Chirurgery.

All which he eloquently reckons up,
That she might know how great a God he was:
And being charm'd with *Cupid's* golden cup
He partiallie unto her praise doth passe,
Calling her tipe of honour, Queen of beauty:
To whom all eies owe tributary duety.   90

I loved once, (quoth hee) aie me I lov'd,
As faire a shape as ever nature framed:
Had she not been so hard t'have been remov'd,
By birth a sea-Nymph; cruell *Daphne* named:
Whom, for shee would not to my will agree,
The Gods transform'd into a Laurell tree.

Ah therfore be not, (with that word he kist her)
Be not (quot he) so proud as *Daphne* was:
Ne care thou for the anger of my sister,
She cannot, nay she shall not hurt my *Cass:*   100
For if she doe, I vow (by dreadfull night)
Never againe to lend her of my light.

This said: he sweetly doth imbrace his love,
Yoaking his armes about her Ivory necke:
And calls her wanton *Venus* milk-white Dove,
Whose ruddie lips the damaske roses decke.
And ever as his tongue compiles her praise,
Love daintie Dimples in her cheekes doth raise.

And meaning now to worke her stratagem
Upon the silly God, that thinks none ill,   110
She hugs him in her armes, and kisses him;
(Th'easlyer to intice him to her will.)
And being not able to maintaine the feeld,
Thus she begins (or rather seemes) to yeeld.

Woon with thy words, and ravisht with thy beauty,
Loe here *Cassandra* yeelds her selfe to thee,
Requiring nothing for thy vowed duety,
But only firmnesse, Love, and secrecy:
Which for that now (even now) I meane to try thee,
A boone I crave; which thou canst not deny me.   120

Scarce were these honywords breath'd from her lips,
But he, supposing that she ment good-faith,
Her filed tongues temptations interceps;
And (like a Novice,) thus to her he saith:

Aske what thou wilt, and I will give it thee,
Health, wealth, long life, wit, art, or dignitie.

Here-with she blushing red, (for shame did adde
A crimson tincture to her palish hew,)
Seeming in outward semblance passing glad,
(As one that th'end of her petition knew)   130
She makes him sweare by ugly *Acheron,*
That he his promise should performe anon.

Which done: relying on his sacred oath,
She askes of him the gift of prophecie:
He (silent) gives consent: though seeming loath
To grant so much to fraile mortalitie:
But since that he his vowes maie not recall,
He gives to her the sp'rite propheticall.

But she no sooner had obtain'd her wish,
When straite unpris'ning her lascivious armes   140
From his softe bosom (th'alvary of blisse)
She chastely counterchecks loves hote alarmes:
And fearing lest his presence might offend her,
She slips aside; and (absent) doth defend her.

(Muliere ne credas, ne mortuae quidem.)

Looke how a brightsome Planet in the skie,
(Spangling the Welkin with a golden spot)
Shootes suddenly from the beholders eie,
And leaves him looking there where she is not:

Even so amazed *Phoebus* (to descrie her)
Lookes all about, but no where can espie her.   150

Not th'hungry Lyon, having lost his pray,
With greater furie runneth through the wood,
(Making no signe of momentarie staie
Till he have satisfi'd himselfe with blood,)
Then angry *Phoebus* mounts into the skie:
Threatning the world with his hot-burning eie.

Now nimbly to his glist'ring Coach he skips,
And churlishlie ascends his loftie chaire,
Yerking his head strong Jades with yron whips,
Whose fearefull neighing ecchoes through the aire,   160
Snorting out fierie Sulphure from their nosethrils:
Whose deadly damp the worlds poore people kils.

Him leave me (for a while) amids the heavens,
Wreaking his anger on his sturdie steedes:
Whose speedful course the day and night now eevens,
(The earth dis-robed of her summer weedes)
And nowe black-mantled night with her browne vaile,
Covers each thing that all the world might quaile.

When loe, *Cassandra* lying at her rest,
(Her rest were restlesse thoughts:) it so befell,   170
Her minde with multitude of cares opprest,
Requir'd some sleepe her passions to expell:
Which when sad *Morpheus* well did understand,
He clos'd her eie-lids with his leaden hand.

Now sleepeth shee: and as shee sleepes, beholde;
Shee seems to see the God whom late shee wronged
Standing before her; whose fierce looks unfold,
His hidden wrath (to whom just ire belonged)
Seeing, shee sighs, and sighing quak't for feare,
To see the shaddow of her shame appeare.   180

Betwixt amaze and dread as shee thus stands,
The fearefull vision drew more neere unto her:
And pynioning her armes in captive bands
So sure, that mortall wight may not undoe her,
He with a bloudy knife (oh cruell part,)
With raging fury stabd her to the heart.

Heerewith awaking from her slumbring sleepe,
(For feare, and care, are enemies to rest:)
At such time as *Aurora* gins to peepe
And shew her selfe; far orient in the East: 190
Shee heard a voice which said: O wicked woman,
Why dost thou stil the gods to vengeance summon?

Thou shalt (indeede) fore-tell of things to come;
And truely, too; (for why my vowes are past)
But heare the end of *Joves* eternall doome:
Because thy promise did so little last,
Although thou tell the truth, (this gift I give thee)
Yet for thy falsehood, no man shall beleeve thee.

And (for thy sake) this pennance I impose
Upon the remnant of all woman kinde,   200
For that they be such truth professed foes;
A constant woman shall be hard to finde:

And that all flesh at my dread name may tremble,
When they weep most, then shall they most dissemble.

This said *Apollo* then: And since that time
His words have proved true as Oracles:
Whose turning thoughtes ambitiously doe clime
To heavens height; and world with lightnes fils:
Whose sex are subject to inconstancie,
As other creatures are to destinie.   210

Yet famous *Sabrine* on thy banks doth rest
The fairest Maide that ever world admired:
Whose constant minde, with heavenly gifts possest,
Makes her rare selfe of all the world desired.
In whose chaste thoughts no vanitie doth enter;
So pure a minde *Endymions* Love hath lent her.

Queene of my thoughts, but subject of my verse,
(Divine *Eliza)* pardon my defect:
Whose artlesse pen so rudely doth reherse
Thy beauties worth; (for want of due respect)   220
Oh pardon thou the follies of my youth;
Pardon my faith, my love, my zeale, my truth.

But to *Cassandra* now: who having heard
The cruell sentence of the threatening voice;
At length (too late) begins to waxe affeard,
Lamenting much her unrepentant choice:
And seeing her hard hap without reliefe,
She sheeds salt teares in token of her griefe.

Which when *Aurora* saw, and saw t'was shee,
Even shee her selfe whose far-renowned fame   230
Made all the world to wonder at her beauty,
It mov'd compassion in this ruthfull Dame:
And thinking on her Sonnes sad destinie,
With mournfull teares she beares her companie.

Great was the mone, which faire *Cassandra* made:
Greater the kindnesse, which *Aurora* shew'd:
Whose sorrow with the sunne began to fade
And her moist teares on th'earths green grasse bestow'd:
Kissing the flowers with her silver dew,
Whose fading beautie, seem'd her case to rew.   240

Scarce was the lovely Easterne Queene departed,
From stately *Ilion;* (whose proud-reared wals
Seem'd to controule the cloudes, till *Vulcan* darted
Against their Towers his burning fier-bals)
When sweet *Cassandra* (leaving her soft bed)
In seemely sort her selfe appareled.

And hearing that her honourable Sire,
(Old princely *Pryamus Troy's* aged King)
Was gone into *Joves* Temple, to conspire
Against the *Greekes,* (whom he to war did bring)   250
Shee, (like a Furie) in a bedlam rage,
Runs gadding thither, his fell wrath t'assuage.

But not prevailing: truely she fore-tolde
The fall of *Troy,* (with bold erected face:)
They count her hare-brain'd, mad, and over-bold,
To presse in presence in so grave a place:

But in meane season *Paris* he is gone,
To bring destruction on faire *Ilion.*

What, ten-yeeres siedge by force could not subvert,
That, two false traitors in one night destroi'd: 260
Who richly guerdon'd for their bad desert,
Was of *Aeneas* but small time injoi'd:
Who, for concealement of *Achilles* love,
Was banished; from *Ilion* to remove.

King *Pryam* dead and all the Trojans slaine;
(His sonnes, his friends and deere confederates)
And lots now cast for captives that remaine,
(Whom Death hath spared for more cruell fates)
Cassandra then to *Agamemnon* fell,
With whom a Lemman she disdain'd to dwell.   270

She, weepes; he, wooes; he would, but she would not:
He, tells his birth; shee, pleades virginitie:
He saith, selfe-pride doth rarest beauty blot:
(And with that word he kist her lovingly:)
Shee, yeeldingly resists; he faines to die:
Shee, falls for feare; he, on her feareleslie.

But this brave generall of all the *Greekes,*
Was quickly foyled at a womans hands,
For who so rashly such incounters seekes,
Of hard mis-hap in danger ever stands: 280
Onely chaste thoughts, and vertuous abstinence,
Gainst such sweet poyson is the sur'st defence.

But who can shun the force of beauties blow?
Who is not ravisht with a lovely looke?
Grac'd with a wanton eie, (the hearts dumb show)
Such fish are taken with a silver hooke:
And when true love cannot these pearles obtaine,
Unguentum Album is the only meane.

Farre be it from my thought (divinest Maid)
To have relation to thy heavenly hew,   290
(In whose sweete voice the Muses are imbaid)
No pen can paint thy commendations due:
Save only that pen, which no pen can be,
An Angels quill, to make a pen for thee.

But to returne to these unhappie Lovers,
(Sleeping securely in each others armes,)
Whose sugred joies nights sable mantle covers,
Little regarding their ensuing harmes:
Which afterward they jointlie both repented:
"Fate is fore-seene, but never is prevented."   300

Which saying to be true, this lucklesse Dame
Approved in the sequele of her story:
Now waxing pale, now blushing red (for shame),
She seales her lips with silence, (womens glory)
Till *Agamemnon* urging her replies,
Thus of his death she truely prophecies.

The day shall come, (quoth she) O dismall daie!
When thou by false *Aegistus* shalt be slaine:
Heere could she tell no more; but made a stay.
(From further speech as willing to refraine:)   310

Not knowing then, nor little did she thinke,
That she with him of that same cup must drinke.

But what? (fond man) he laughes her skil to scorne,
And jesteth at her divination:
Ah to what unbeliefe are Princes borne?
(The onely over-throw of many a Nation:)
And so it did befall this lucklesse Prince,
Whom all the world hath much lamented since.

Insteede of teares, he smileth at her tale:
Insteede of griefe, he makes great shew of gladnes: 320
But after blisse, there ever followes bale;
And after mirth, there alwaies commeth sadnes:
But gladnesse, blisse, and mirth had so possest him,
That sadnes, bale, and griefe could not molest him.

Oh cruell *Parcae* (quoth *Cassandra* then)
Why are you *Parcae*, yet not mov'd with praier?
Oh small security of mortall men,
That live on earth, and breathe this vitall aire:
When we laugh most, then are we next to sorrow;
The Birds feede us to-day, we them to-morrow.   330

But if the first did little move his minde,
Her later speeches lesse with him prevailed;
Who beinge wholy to selfe-will inclinde,
Deemes her weake braine with lunacy assailed:
And still the more shee councels him to stay,
The more he striveth to make haste away.

How on the Seas he scap'd stormes, rocks and sholes,
(Seas that envide the conquest he had wone,
Gaping like hell to swallow Greekish soules,)
I heere omit; onely suppose it done: 340
His storm-tyrde Barke safely brings him to shore,
His whole Fleete els, or suncke or lost before.

Lift up thy head, thou ashie-cyndred *Troy*,
See the commaunder of thy traitor foes,
That made thy last nights woe, his first daies joie,
Now gins his night of joy and daie of woes:
His fall be thy delight, thine was his pride:
As he thee then, so now thou him deride.

He and *Cassandra* now are set on shore
Which he salutes with joy, she greetes with teares,   350
Currors are sent that poast to Court before,
Whose tidings fill th'adultrous Queene with feares,
Who with *Aegistus* in a lust-staind bed,
Her selfe, her King, her State dishonored.

She wakes the lecher with a loud-strain'd shrike,
Love-toies they leave, now doth lament begin:
Ile flie (quoth he) but she doth that mislike,
Guilt unto guilt, and sinne she ads to sinne:
Shee meanes to kill (immodest love to cover)
A kingly husband, for a caytive lover.   360

The peoples joies, conceived at his returne,
Their thronging multitudes: their gladsome cries,
Their gleeful hymnes, whiles piles of incense burne:
Their publique shewes, kept at solemnitics:

We passe: and tell how King and Queene did meet,
Where he with zeale, she him with guile did greet.

He (noble Lord) fearelesse of hidden treason,
Sweetely salutes this weeping Crocodile:
Excusing every cause with instant reason
That kept him from her sight so long a while: 370
She, faintly pardons him; smiling by Art:
(For life was in her lookes, death in her hart.)

For pledge that I am pleas'd receive (quoth shee,)
This rich wrought robe, thy *Clytemnestraes* toile:
Her ten yeeres worke this day shall honour thee,
For ten yeeres war, and one daies glorious spoile:
Whil'st thou contendedst there, I heere did this:
Weare it my love, my life, my joy, my blisse.

Scarce had the Syren said, what I have write,
But he (kind Prince) by her milde words misled,   380
Receiv'd the robe, to trie if it were fit;
(The robe) that had no issue for his head;
Which, whilst he vainly hoped to have found,
Aegistus pierst him with a mortal wound.

Oh how the *Troyan* Damzell was amazed,
To see so fell and bloudy a Tragedie,
Performed in one Act; she naught but gazed,
Upon the picture; whom shee dead did see,
Before her face: whose body she emballms,
With brennish teares, and sudden deadly qualms.   390

Faine would she have fled backe on her swift horse,
But *Clytemnestra* bad her be content,
Her time was com'n: now bootelesse us'd she force,
Against so many; whom this Tygresse sent
To apprehend her: who (within one hower
Brought backe againe) was lockt within a Tower.

Now is she joylesse, friendlesse, and (in fine)
Without all hope of further libertie:
Insteed of cates, cold water was her wine,
And *Agamemnons* corps her meate must be,   400
Or els she must for hunger starve (poore sole)
What could she do but make great mone and dole.

So darke the dungeon was, wherein she was,
That neither Sunne (by day) nor Mone (by night)
Did shew themselves: and thus it came to passe.
The Sunne denide to lend his glorious light
To such a perjur'd wight, or to be seene;
(What neede she light, that over-light had bin?)

Now silent night drew on; when all things sleepe,
Save theeves, and cares; and now stil mid-night came: 410
When sad *Cassandra* did naught els but weepe;
Oft calling on her *Agamemnons* name.
But seeing that the dead did not replie,
Thus she begins to mourne, lament, and crie.

Oh cruell Fortune, (mother of despaire,)
Well art thou christen'd with a cruell name:
Since thou regardest not the wise, or faire,
But do'st bestow thy riches (to thy shame)

On fooles and lowly swaines, that care not for thee:
And yet I weepe, and yet thou do'st abhorre me.   420

Fie on ambition, fie on filthy pride,
The roote of ill, the cause of all my woe:
On whose fraile yce my youth first slipt aside:
And falling downe, receiv'd a fatall blow.
Ah who hath liv'd to see such miserie
As I have done, and yet I cannot die?

I liv'd (quoth she) to see *Troy* set on fire:
I liv'd to see, renowned *Hector* slaine:
I liv'd to see, the shame of my desire:
And yet I live, to feele more grievous paine: 430
Let all young maides example take by me,
To keepe their oathes, and spotlesse chastity.

Happy are they, that never liv'd to know
What t'is to live in this world happily:
Happy are they which never yet felt woe:
Happy are they, that die in infancie:
Whose sins are cancell'd in their mothers wombe:
Whose cradle is their grave, whose lap their tomb.

Here ended shee; and then her teares began,
That (Chorus-like) at every word downe rained.   440
Which like a paire of christall fountaines ran,
Along her lovely cheekes: with roses stained:
Which as they wither still (for want of raine)
Those silver showers water them againe.

Now had the pore-mans clock (shrill chauntcleare)
Twice given notice of the Mornes approach,
(That then began in glorie to appeare,
Drawne in her stately colour'd saffron-Coach)
When shee (poore Lady) almost turn'd to teares,
Began to teare and rend her golden haires.   450

Lie there (quoth shee) the workers of my woes;
You trifling toies, which my lives staine have bin:
You, by whose meanes our coines chiefly growes,
Clothing the backe with pride, the soule with sin:
Lie there (quoth shee) the causers of my care;
This said, her robes she all in pieces tare.

Here-with, as weary of her wretched life,
(Which she injoyd with small felicitie)
She ends her fortune with a fatall knife;
(First day of joy, last day of miserie:)   460
Then why is death accounted Nature's foe,
Since death (indeed) is but the end of woe?

For as by death, her bodie was released
From that strong prison made of lime and stone;
Even so by death her purest soule was eased,
From bodies prison, and from endlesse mone:
Where now shee walkes in sweete *Elysium*,
(The place for wrongful Death and Martirdum.)

Finis.

The Encomion of Lady Pecunia:
or
The Praise of Money.

**—quaerenda pecunia primum est,
Virtus post nummos. Horace.**

By Richard Barnfeild,
Graduate in Oxford.

London,
Printed by G. S. John Jaggard, and are to
be sold at his shoppe neere Temple-barre, at the
Signe of the Hand and starre.
1598

[The Authors First Epistle-Dedicatory.   [1605 ed.]

Led by the swift report of winged Fame,
With silver trumpet, sounding forth your name
To you I dedicate this merry Muse,
And for my Patron, I your favour chuse:
She is a Lady, she must be respected:
She is a Queene, she may not be neglected.
This is the shadow, you the substance have,
Which substance now this shadow seems to crave.

    Richard Barnfield.]

To the Gentlemen Readers.

Gentlemen, being incouraged through your gentle acceptance of my *Cynthia*, I have once more adventured on your Curtesies: hoping to finde you (as I have done heretofore) friendly. Being determined to write of somthing, and yet not resolved of any thing, I considered with myselfe, if one should write of Love (they will say) why, every one writes of Love: if of Vertue, why, who regards Vertue? To be short, I could thinke of nothing, but either it was common, or not at all in request. At length I bethought my selfe of a Subject, both new (as having never beene written upon before) and pleasing (as I thought) because Mans Nature (commonly) loves to heare that praised, with whose pressence, hee is most pleased.

Erasmus (the glory of *Netherland,* and the refiner of the Latin Tongue) wrote a whole Booke, in *the prayse of Folly.* Then if so excellent a Scholler, writ in praise of Vanity, why may not I write in praise of that which is profitable? There are no two Countreys, where Gold is esteemed, lesse than in *India,* and more then in *England:* the reason is, because the *Indians* are barbarous, and our Nation civill.

I have given *Pecunia* the title of a Woman, Both for the termination of the Word, and because (as Women are) shee is lov'd of men. The bravest Voyages in the World, have beene made for Gold: for it, men have venterd (by Sea) to the furthest parts of the Earth: In the Pursute whereof, *Englands Nestor* and *Neptune (Haukins* and *Drake)* lost their lives. Upon the Deathes of the which two, of the first I writ this:

The Waters were his Winding Sheete, the Sea was made his Toome;
Yet for his fame the Ocean Sea, was not sufficient roome.

Of the latter this:

England his hart; his Corps the Waters have;
And that which raysd his fame, became his grave.

The *Praetorians* (after the death of *Pertinax*) in the election of a new Emperour, more esteemed the money of *Julianus*, than either the vertue of *Severus*, or the Valour of *Pessennius*. Then of what great estimation and account, this Lady *Pecunia*, both hath beene in the Worlde, and is at this present, I leave to your Judgement. But what speake I so much of her praise in my Epistle, that have commended her so at large in my Booke? To the reading whereof, (Gentlemen) I referre you.

The Prayse of Lady Pecunia

I sing not of *Angellica* the faire,
(For whom the Palladine of *Fraunce* fell mad)
Nor of sweet *Rosamond,* olde *Cliffords* heire,
(Whose death did make the second *Henry* sad)
But of the fairest Faire *Pecunia,*
The famous Queene of rich *America.*

Goddesse of Golde, great Empresse of the Earth,
O thou that canst doo all Things under Heaven:
That doost convert the saddest minde to Mirth;
(Of whom the elder Age was quite bereaven)   10
Of thee Ile sing, and in thy Prayse Ile write;
You *golden Angels* helpe me to indite.

You, you alone, can make my Muse to speake;
And tell a golden Tale, with silver Tongue:
You onely can my pleasing silence breake;
And adde some Musique, to a merry Songue:
But amongst all the five, in Musicks Art,
I would not sing the *Counter*-tenor part.

The Meane is best, and that I meane to keepe;
So shall I keepe my selfe from That I meane: 20
Lest with some Others, I be forc'd to weepe,
And cry *Peccavi*, in a dolefull Scaene.
But to the matter which I have in hand,
The Lady Regent, both by Sea and Land.

When *Saturne* liv'd, and wore the Kingly Crowne,
(And *Jove* was yet unborne, but not unbred)
This Ladies fame was then of no renowne;
(For Golde was then, no more esteem'd then Lead)
Then Truth and Honesty were onely us'd,
Silver and Golde were utterly refus'd.   30

But when the Worlde grew wiser in Conceit,
And saw how Men in manners did decline,
How Charitie began to loose her heate,
And One did at anothers good repine,
Then did the Aged, first of all respect her;
And vowd from thencefoorth, never to reject her.

Thus with the Worlde, her beauty did increase,
And manie Suters had she to obtaine her:
Some sought her in the Wars, and some in peace;
But few of youthfull age, could ever gaine her: 40
Or if they did, she soone was gone againe;
And would with them, but little while remaine.

For why against the Nature of her Sexe,
(That commonlie dispise the feeble Olde)
Shee, loves olde men; but young men she rejects;
Because to her, their Love is quicklie colde:
Olde men (like Husbands jealous of their Wives)
Lock her up fast, and keepe her as their Lives.

The young man carelesse to maintaine his life,
Neglects her Love (as though he did abhor her)   50
Like one that hardly doeth obtaine a wife,
And when he hath her once, he cares not for her:
Shee, seeing that the young man doeth despyse her,
Leaves the franke heart, and flies unto the Myser.

Hee intertaines her, with a joyfull hart;
And seemes to rue her undeserved wrong:
And from his Pressence, she shall never part;
Or if shee doo, he thinkes her Absence long:
And oftentimes he sends for her againe,
Whose life without her, cannot long remaine.   60

And when he hath her, in his owne possession,
He locks her in an iron-barred Chest,
And doubting somewhat, of the like Transgression.
He holds that iron-walled prison best.
And least some *rusty* sicknesse should infect her,
He often visits her, and doeth respect her.

As for the young man (subject unto sinne)
No marvell though the Divell doe distresse him;
To tempt mans frailtie, which doth never linne,
Who many times, hath not a *Crosse* to blesse him: 70
But how can hee incurre the Heavens Curse,
That hath so many *Crosses* in his Purse?

Hee needes not feare those wicked sprights, that waulke
Under the Coverture of cole-blacke Night;
For why the Divell still, a *Crosse* doeth baulke,
Because on it, was hangd the Lorde of Light:
But let not Mysers trust to *silver Crosses*,
Least in the End, their gaines be turnd to losses.

But what care they, so they may hoorde up golde?
Either for God, or Divell, or Heaven, or hell?   80
So they may faire *Pecuniaes* face behold;
And every Day, their Mounts of Money tell.
What tho to count their Coyne, they never blin,
Count they their Coyne, and counts not God their sin?

But what talke I of sinne, to Usurers?
Or looke for mendment, at a Mysers hand?
Pecunia, hath so many followers,
Bootlesse it is, her Power to with-stand.
King *Covetise*, and *Warinesse* his Wife,
The Parents were, that first did give her Life.   90

But now unto her Praise I will proceede,
Which is as ample, as the Worlde is wide:
What great Contentment doth her Pressence breede
In him, that can his wealth with Wysdome guide?
She is the Soveraigne Queene, of all Delights:
For her the Lawyer pleades; the Souldier fights.

For her, the Merchant venters on the Seas:
For her, the Scholler studdies at his Booke:
For her, the Usurer (with greater ease)
For sillie fishes, layes a silver hooke: 100
For her, the Townsman leaves the Countrey Village:
For her, the Plowman gives himselfe to Tillage.

For her, the Gentleman doeth raise his rents:
For her, the Servingman attends his maister:
For her, the curious head new toyes invents:
For her, to Sores, the Surgeon layes his plaister.
In fine for her, each man in his Vocation,
Applies himselfe, in everie sev'rall Nation.

What can thy hart desire, but thou mayst have it,
If thou hast readie money to disburse?   110
Then thanke thy Fortune, that so freely gave it;
For of all friends, the surest is thy purse.
Friends may prove false, and leave thee in thy need;
But still thy Purse will bee thy friend indeed.

Admit thou come, into a place unknowne;
And no man knowes, of whence, or what thou art:
If once thy faire *Pecunia*, shee be showne,
Thou art esteem'd a man of great Desart:
And placed at the Tables upper ende;
Not for thine owne sake, but thy faithfull frende.   120

But if you want your Ladies lovely grace,
And have not wherewithall to pay your shot,
Your Hostis pressently will step in Place,
You are a Stranger (Sir) I know you not:
By trusting Divers, I am run in Det;
Therefore of mee, nor meate nor Bed you get.

O who can then, expresse the worthie praise,
Which faire *Pecunia* justly doeth desarve?
That can the meanest man, to Honor raise;
And feed the soule, that ready is to starve.   130
Affection, which was wont to bee so pure,
Against a golden Siege, may not endure.

Witnesse the trade of Mercenary sinne;
(Or Occupation, if thou list to tearme it)
Where faire *Pecunia* must the suite beginne;
(As common-tride Experience doeth confirme it)
Not *Mercury* himselfe, with silver Tongue,
Can so inchaunt, as can a golden Songue.

When nothing could subdue the *Phrygian Troy,*
(That Citty through the world so much renowned)   140
Pecunia did her utterly destroy:
And left her fame, in darke Oblivion drowned.
And many Citties since, no lesse in fame,
For Love of her, have yeelded to their shame.

What Thing is then, so well belov'd as money?
It is a speciall Comfort to the minde;
More faire then Women are; more sweet than honey:
Easie to loose, but very harde to finde.
In fine, to him, whose Purse beginns to faint,
Golde is a God, and silver is a Saint.   150

The Tyme was once, when Honestie was counted
A Demy god; and so esteem'd of all:
But now *Pecunia* on his Seate is mounted;
Since Honestie in great Disgrace did fall.
No state, no Calling now, doeth him esteeme;
Nor of the other ill, doeth any deeme.

The reason is, because he is so poore:
(And who respects the poore, and needie Creature?)
Still begging of his almes, from Doore to Doore:
All ragd, and torne; and eeke deformed in feature.   160
In Countinance so changde, that none can know him;
So weake, that every vice doeth overthrow him.

But faire *Pecunia*, (most divinely bred)
For sundrie shapes, doth *Proteus* selfe supasse:
In one Lande, she is suted all in Lead;
And in another, she is clad in Brasse:
But still within the Coast of *Albion*,
She ever puts, her best Apparell on.

Silver and Golde, and nothing else is currant,
In *Englands*, in faire *Englands* happy Land: 170
All baser sorts of Mettalls, have no Warrant;
Yet secretly they *slip*, from hand to hand.
If any such be tooke, the same is lost,
And pressently is nayled on a Post.

Which with Quick-silver, being flourisht over,
Seemes to be perfect Silver, to the showe:
As Woemens paintings, their defects doe cover,
Under this false attyre, so doe they goe.
If on a woolen Cloth, thou rub the same,
Then will it straight beginne to blush, for shame.   180

If chafed on thy haire, till it be hot,
If it good Silver bee, the scent is sweete:
If counterfeit, thy chafing hath begot
A ranke-smelt savour; for a Queene unmeete:
Pecunia is a Queene, for her Desarts,
And in the Decke, may goe for *Queene of harts*.

The Queene of harts, because she rules all harts;
And hath all harts, obedient to her Will:
Whose Bounty, fame unto the Worlde imparts;
And with her glory, all the Worlde doeth fill: 190

The *Queene of Diamonds,* she cannot bee;
There is but one, ELIZA, thou art shee.

And thou art shee, O sacred Soveraigne;
Whom God hath helpt with his Al-mighty hand:
Blessing thy People, with thy peacefull raigne;
And made this little Land, a happy Land:
May all those live, that wish long life to thee,
And all the rest, perish eternally.

Thy tyme was once, when faire *Pecunia,* here
Did basely goe attyred all in Leather: 200
But since her raigne, she never did appeare
But richly clad; in Golde, or Silver either:
Nor reason is it, that her Golden raigne
With baser Coyne, eclypsed should remaine.

And as the Coyne, she hath repurifyde,
From baser substance, to the purest Mettels:
Religion so, hath shee refinde beside,
From Papistrie, to Truth; which daily settles
Within her Peoples harts; though some there bee,
That cleave unto their wonted Papistrie.   210

No flocke of sheepe, but some are still infected:
No peece of Lawne so pure, but hath some fret:
All buildings are not strong, that are erected:
All Plants prove not, that in good ground are set:
Some tares are sowne, amongst the choicest seed:
No garden can be cleansd of every Weede.

[But now more Angels than on Earth yet weare   [1605 ed.]
Her golden Impresse; have to Heaven attended
Hir Virgin-soule; now, now she sojornes there,
Tasting more joyes then may be comprehended.

Life, she hath changde for life (oh countless gaine)
An earthlie rule, for an eternall Raigne.

Such a Successor leaving in her stead,
So peerlesse worthie, and so Royall wise;
In him her virtues live, though she be dead:
Bountie and zeale, in him both soveranize.
To him alone, Pecunia doth obay,
He ruling her, that doth all others sway.

Bounty, that when she sickned, cras'd and fainted,
And when she left the earth had almost died;
Hoping with her, in heaven to have bin sainted,
And monst the rest an Angels place supplyed:
This King hath cherisht, and his life assured,
And of a long consumption, Bounti's cured.

Plenty and Peace upon his Throne attend,
Health and Content, upon his person wait:
Conquest and Fame, his Royaltie defend,
May all good Planets smile upon his state,
By whom all-drooping-vertues are revived,
And dying-Bounty, made againe long lived.

The hand of Heaven still take him to his keeping,
Him, in no danger, in no doubt forsaking;
A thousand of his Angels guarde him sleeping,
And all the hoast of heaven protect him waking.
That he in safety, peace and rest, may raigne,
Whilst the two Poles, the frame of heven sustain.]

But now to her, whose praise is here pretended,
(Divine *Pecunia*) fairer then the morne:
Which cannot be sufficiently commended;
Whose Sun-bright Beauty doeth the Worlde adorne,   220

Adorns the World, but specially the Purse;
Without whose pressence, nothing can be woorse.

Not faire *Haesione* (King of *Priams* sister)
Did ever showe more Beauty, in her face,
Then can this lovely Lady, if it list her
To showe her selfe; admir'd for comely grace:
Which neither Age can weare, not Tyme conclude;
For why, her Beauty yeerely is renude.

[New Coine is yearlie stamped in the Tower,   [1605 ed.]
But these faire daies of joy, addes alteration:
In faire Elizaes raign, none had that power;
But kingly glorie, clothes her new in fashion,
Ads beautie to her beames, by adding more
Then grayest haires in life, ere saw before.]

New Coyne is coynd each yeare, within the Tower
So that her Beauty never can decay: 230
Which to resist, no mortall man hath Power,
When as she doeth her glorious Beames display.
Nor doeth *Pecunia,* onely please the eie,
But charms the eare, with heavenly Harmonie.

[Stand forth who can and tell, and truelie saie   [1605 ed.]
When England, Scotland, Ireland and France,
He ever saw Pecunia to displaie
Before these daies; O wondrous happie chance.
Nor doth Pecunia onelie please the eie,
But charmes the eare, with heavenlie harmony.]

Lyke to an other *Orpheus,* can she play
Upon her *treble Harpe,* whose silver sound
Inchaunts the eare, and steales the hart away:
Nor hardly can deceit, therein be found.

Although such Musique, some a Shilling cost,
Yet is it worth but *Nine-pence,* at the most.   240

[But Ireland alone, this Musicks sound   [1605 ed.]
Being clad in Silver, challenge for their coine,
What though amongst us much thereof be found,
Authoritie, no subject dooth injoyne
Above his worth to countenance the same,
Then men, not coin, are worthy of that blame.]

Had I the sweet inchaunting Tongue of *Tully,*
That charmd the hearers, lyke the Syrens Song;
Yet could I not describe the Prayses fully,
Which to *Pecunia* justly doe belong.
Let it suffice, her Beauty doeth excell:
Whose praise no Pen can paint, no Tongue can tell.

Then how shall I describe, with artlesse Pen,
The praise of her, whose praise, all praise surmounteth?
Breeding amazement, in the mindes of men:
Of whom, this pressent Age so much accounteth.   250
Varietie of Words would sooner want,
Then store of plentious matter, would be scant.

Whether yee list, to looke into the Citty:
(Where money tempts the poore Beholders eye)
Or to the Countrey Townes, devoyde of Pitty:
(Where to the poore, each place doeth almes denye)
All Thinges for money now, are bought and solde,
That either hart can thinke, or eie beholde.

Nay more for money (as report doeth tell)
Thou mayst obteine a pardon for thy sinnes: 260
The Pope of *Rome,* for money will it sell;
(Whereby thy soule, no small salvation winnes)

But how can hee (of Pride the chiefe Beginner)
Forgive thy sinnes, that is himselfe a sinner?

Then, sith the Pope is subject unto sinne,
No marvell tho, divine *Pecunia* tempt him,
With her faire Beauty; whose good-will to winne,
Each one contends; and shall we then exempt him.
Did never mortall man, yet looke upon her,
But straightwaies he became, enamourd on her.   270

Yet would I wish, the Wight that loves her so,
And hath obtain'd, the like good-will againe,
To use her wisely, lest she prove his foe;
And so, in stead of Pleasure, breed his paine.
She may be kyst, but shee must not be *clypt*:
Lest such Delight in bitter gall be dypt.

The juyce of grapes, which is a soveraigne Thing
To cheere the hart, and to revive the spirits;
Being usde immoderatly (in surfetting)
Rather Dispraise, then commendation merits: 280
Even so *Pecunia*, is, as shee is used;
Good of her selfe, but bad if once abused.

With her, the Tenant payes his Landlords rent:
On her, depends the stay of every state:
To her, rich Pressents every day are sent:
In her, it rests to end all dire Debate:
Through her, to Wealth, is raisd the Countrey Boore:
From her, proceedes much proffit to the poore.

Then how can I, sufficiently commend,
Her Beauties worth, which makes the World to wonder?   290
Or end her prayse, whose prayses have no End?
Whose absence brings the stoutest stomack under:

Let it suffice, *Pecunia* hath no peere;
No Wight, no Beauty held; more faire, more deere.

Finis

His Prayer to Pecunia

Great Lady, sith I have complyde thy Prayse,
(According to my skill and not thy merit)
And sought thy Fame above the starrs to rayse;
(Had I sweet *Ovids* vaine, or *Virgils* spirit)
I crave no more but this, for my good will,
That in my Want, thou wilt supplye me still.

The Complaint of Poetrie, for the Death of Liberalitie.

Vivit post funera virtus.

London,
Printed by G.S. for John Jaggard, and are to
be solde at his shoppe neere Temple-barre, at the
Signe of the Hand and starre.
1598.

To his Worshipfull wel-willer, Maister
Edward Leigh, of Grayes Inne.

Image of that, whose losse is here lamented;
(In whom, so many vertues are contained)
Daine to accept, what I have now presented.
Though Bounties death, herein be only fained,
If in your mind, she not revive (with speed)
Then will I sweare, that shee is dead indeed.

The Complaint of
Poetrie, for the Death
of Liberalitie.

Weepe Heavens now, for you have lost your light;
Ye Sunne and Moone, beare witnes of my mone:
The cleere is turnd to clouds; the day to night;
And all my hope, and all my joy is gone:
Bounty is dead, the cause of my annoy;
Bounty is dead, and with her dide my joy.

O who can comfort my afflicted soule?
Or adde some ende to my increasing sorrowes?
Who can deliver me from endlesse dole?
(Which from my hart eternall torment borrowes.)   10
When *Bounty* liv'd, I bore the Bell away;
When *Bounty* dide, my credit did decay.

I never then, did write one verse in vaine;
Nor ever went my Poems unregarded:

Then did each Noble breast, me intertaine,
And for my Labours I was well rewarded;
But now *Good wordes,* are stept in *Bounties* place,
Thinking thereby, her glorie to disgrace.

But who can live with words, in these hard tymes?
(Although they came from *Jupiter* himselfe?)   20
Or who can take such Paiment, for his Rymes?
(When nothing now, is so esteem'd as Pelfe?)
Tis not *Good wordes,* that can a man maintaine;
Wordes are but winde; and winde is all but vaine.

Where Is *Mecaenas,* Learnings noble Patron?
(That *Maroes* Muse, with Bountie so did cherish?)
Or faire *Zenobia,* that worthy Matron?
(Whose name, for Learnings love, shall never perish.)
What tho their Bodies, lie full lowe in grave,
Their fame the worlde; their souls the Heavens have.   30

Vile *Avaricia,* how hast thou inchaunted
The Noble mindes, of great and mightie Men?
Or what infernall furie late hath haunted
Their niggard Purses? (to the learned pen)
Was it *Augustus* wealth, or noble minde,
That everlasting fame, to him assinde?

If wealth? Why *Croesus* was more rich then hee;
(Yet *Croesus* glorie, with his life did end)
It was his Noble mind, that moved mee
To write his praise, and eeke his Acts commend.   40
Who ere had heard, of *Alexanders* fame,
If *Quintus Curtius* had not pend the same?

Then sith by mee, their deedes have been declared,
(Which else had perisht with their lives decay)

Who to augment their glories, have not spared
To crowne their browes, with never-fading Bay:
What Art deserves such Liberalitie,
As doeth the peerlesse Art of Poetrie?

But *Liberalitie* is dead and gone:
And *Avarice* usurps true *Bounties* seat,   50
For her it is, I make this endlesse mone,
(Whose praises worth no pen can well repeat)
Sweet *Liberalitie* adiew for ever,
For *Poetrie* againe, shall see thee never.

Never againe, shall I thy presence see:
Never againe, shal I thy bountie tast:
Never againe, shal I accepted bee:
Never againe, shall I be so embrac't:
Never againe, shall I the bad recall:
Never againe, shall I be lov'd of all.   60

Thou wast the Nurse, whose Bountie gave me sucke:
Thou wast the Sunne, whose beames did lend me light:
Thou was the Tree, whose fruit I still did plucke:
Thou wast the Patron, to maintaine my right:
Through thee I liv'd; on thee I did relie;
In thee I joy'd; and now for thee I die.

What man, hath lately lost a faithfull frend?
Or Husband, is deprived of his Wife?
But doth his after-daies in dolour spend?
(Leading a loathsome, discontented life?)   70
Dearer than friend, or wife, have I forgone:
Then marvell not, although I make such mone.

Faire *Philomela,* cease thy sad complaint;
And lend thine eares, unto my dolefull Ditty:

(Whose soule with sorrowe, now begins to faint,
And yet I cannot move mens hearts to pitty:)
Thy woes are light, compared unto mine:
You waterie Nymphes, to mee your plaints resigne.

And thou *Melpomene*, (the Muse of Death)
That never sing'st, but in a dolefull straine;   80
Sith cruell Destinie hath stopt her breath,
(Who whilst she liv'd, was Vertues Soveraigne)
Leave *Hellicon*, (whose bankes so pleasant bee)
And beare a part of sorrowe now with mee.

The Trees (for sorrowe) shead their fading Leaves,
And weepe out gum, in stead of other teares;
Comfort nor joy, no Creature now conceives,
To chirpe and sing, each little bird forbeares.
The sillie Sheepe, hangs downe his drooping head,
And all because, that *Bounty* she is dead.   90

The greater that I feele my griefe to bee,
The lesser able, am I to expresse it;
Such is the nature of extremitie,
The heart it som-thing eases, to confesse it.
Therefore Ile wake my muse, amidst her sleeping,
And what I want in wordes, supplie with weeping.

Weepe still mine eies, a River full of Teares,
To drowne my Sorrowe in, that so molests me;
And rid my head of cares, my thoughts of feares:
Exiling sweet Content, that so detests me.   100
But ah (alas) my Teares are almost dun,
And yet my griefe, it is but new begun.

Even as the Sunne, when as it leaves our sight,
Doth shine with those Antipodes, beneath us;

Lending the other worlde her glorious light,
And dismall Darknesse, onely doeth bequeath us:
Even so sweet *Bountie,* seeming dead to mee,
Lives now to none, but smooth-Tongd Flatterie.

O *Adulation,* Canker-worme of Truth;
The flattring Glasse of Pride, and Self-conceit: 110
(Making olde wrinkled Age, appeare like youth)
Dissimulations Maske, and follies Beate:
Pittie it is, that thou art so rewarded,
Whilst Truth and Honestie, goe unregarded.

O that Nobilitie, it selfe should staine,
In being bountifull, to such vile Creatures:
Who, when they flatter most, then most they faine;
Knowing what humor best, will fit their Natures.
What man so mad, that knowes himselfe but pore,
And will beleeve that he hath riches store.   120

Upon a time, the craftie Foxe did flatter
The foolish Pye (whose mouth was full of meate)
The Pye beleeving him, began to chatter,
And sing for joy, (not having list to eate)
And whil'st the foolish Pye, her meate let fall,
The craftie Foxe, did runne awaie with all.

Terence describeth under *Gnatoes* name,
The right conditions of a Parasyte:
(And with such Eloquence, sets foorth the same,
As doeth the learned Reader much delyght)   130
Shewing, that such a Sycophant as *Gnato,*
Is more esteem'd, then twentie such as *Plato.*

Bounty looke back, upon thy goods mispent;
And thinke how ill, thou hast bestow'd thy mony:

Consider not their wordes, but their intent;
Their hearts are gall, although their tongues be hony:
They speake not as they thinke, but all is fained,
And onely to th'intent to be maintained.

And herein happie, I areade the poore;
No flattring Spanyels, fawne on them for meate: 140
The reason is, because the Countrey Boore
Hath little enough, for himselfe to eate:
No man will flatter him, except himselfe;
And why? because hee hath no store of wealth.

But sure it is not *Liberalitie*
That doeth reward these fawning smel-feasts so:
It is the vice of Prodigalitie,
That doeth the Bankes of *Bounty* over-flo:
Bounty is dead: yea so it needes must bee;
Or if alive, yet is shee dead to mee.   150

Therefore as one, whose friend is lately dead,
I will bewaile the death, of my deere frend;
Uppon whose Tombe, ten thousand Teares Ile shead,
Till drearie Death, of mee shall make an end:
Or if she want a Toombe, to her desart,
Oh then, Ile burie her within my hart.

But *(Bounty)* if thou love a tombe of stone,
Oh then seeke out, a hard and stonie hart:
For were mine so, yet would it melt with mone,
And all because, that I with thee must part.   160
Then, if a stonie hart must thee interr,
Goe finde a Step-dame, or a Usurer.

And sith there dies no Wight, of great account,
But hath an Epitaph compos'd by mee,

Bounty, that did all other far surmount,
Upon her Tombe, this Epitaph shall bee:
Here lies the Wight, that Learning did maintaine,
And at the last by AVARICE was slaine.

Vile *Avarice,* why hast thou kildd my Deare?
And robd the World, of such a worthy Treasure?   170
In whome no sparke of goodnesse doth appeare,
So greedie is thy mind, without all measure,
Thy death, from Death did merit to release her:
The Murtherers deserv'd to die, not *Caesar.*

The Merchants wife; the Tender-hearted Mother:
That leaves her love; whose Sonne is prest for warre;
(Resting, the one; as woefull as the other;)
Hopes yet at length, when ended is the jarre,
To see her Husband; see her Sonne againe:
"Were it not then for Hope, the hart were slaine."   180

But I, whose hope is turned to despaire,
Nere looke to see my dearest Deare againe:
Then *Pleasure* sit thou downe, in *Sorrowes* Chaire,
And (for a while) thy wonted Mirth refraine.
Bounty is dead, that whylome was my Treasure:
Bounty is dead, my joy and onely pleasure.

If *Pythias* death, of *Damon* were bewailed;
Or *Pillades* did rue, *Orestes* ende:
If *Hercules,* for *Hylas* losse were quailed;
Or *Theseus,* for *Pyrithous* Teares did spend: 190
When doe I mourne for *Bounty,* being dead:
Who living, was my hand, my hart, my head.

My hand, to helpe me, in my greatest need:
My hart, to comfort mee, in my distresse:
My head, whom onely I obeyd, indeed:
If she were such, how can my griefe be lesse?
Perhaps My wordes, may pierce the *Parcae's* eares;
If not with wordes, Ile move them with my teares.

But ah (alas) my Teares are spent in vaine,
(For she is dead, and I am left alive)   200
Teares cannot call, sweet *Bounty* backe againe,
Then why doe I, gainst Fate and Fortune strive?
And for her death, thus weepe, lament, and crie;
Sith every mortall wight, is borne to die.

But as the woefull mother doeth lament,
Her tender babe, with cruell Death opprest:
Whose life was spotlesse, pure, and innocent,
(And therefore sure, its soule is gone to rest)
So Bountie, which her selfe did upright keepe,
Yet for her losse, love cannot chuse but weepe.   210

The losse of her, is losse to many a one:
The losse of her, is losse unto the poore:
And therfore not a losse, to mee alone,
But unto such, as goe from Doore to Doore.
Her losse, is losse unto the fatherlesse;
And unto all, that are in great distresse.

The maimed Souldier, comming from the warre,
The woefull wight, whose house was lately burnd;
The sillie soule; the wofull Traveylar;
And all, whom Fortune at her feet hath spurnd   220
Lament the losse of *Liberalitie:*
"Its ease, to have in griefe some Companie."

The Wife of *Hector* (sad *Andromache)*
Did not bewaile, her husbands death alone:
But (sith he was the *Trojans* onely stey)
The wives of *Troy* (for him) made aequall mone.
Shee, shead the teares of Love; and they of pittie:
Shee, for her deare dead Lord; they, for their Cittie.

Nor is the Death of *Liberalitie,*
(Although my griefe be greater than the rest)   230
Onely lamented, and bewaild of mee;
(And yet of mee, she was beloved best)
But, sith she was so bountifull to all,
She is lamented, both of great and small.

O that my Teares could move the powres divine,
That *Bountie* might be calld from the dead:
As Pitty pierc'd the hart of *Proserpine;*
Who (moved with the Teares *Admetus* shead)
Did sende him backe againe, his loving Wife:
Who lost her owne, to save her husbands life.   240

Impartiall *Parcae,* will no prayers move you?
Can Creatures so divine, have stony harts?
Haplesse are they, whose hap it is to prove you,
For you respect no Creatures good Desarts.
O *Atropos,* (the cruelst of the three)
Why hast thou tane, my faithfull friend from mee?

But ah, she cannot (or shee will not) heare me,
Or if shee doo, yet may not she repent her:
Then come (sweet Death) O why doest thou forbeare me?
Aye mee! thy Dart is blunt, it will not enter.   250
Oh now I knowe the cause, and reason why;
I am immortall, and I cannot dye.

So Cytheraea would have dide, but could not;
When faire *Adonis* by her side lay slaine:
So I desire the Sisters, what I should not;
For why (alas) I wish for Death in vaine;
Death is their servant, and obeys their will;
And if they bid him spare, he cannot kill.

Oh would I were, as other Creatures are;
Then would I die, and so my griefe were ended: 260
But Death (against my will) my life doeth spare;
(So little with the fates I am befrended)
Sith, when I would, thou doost my sute denie,
Vile Tyrant, when thou wilt, I will not die.

And *Bounty*, though her body thou hast slain
Yet shall her memorie remaine for ever:
For ever, shall her memorie remaine;
Whereof no spitefull Fortune can bereave her.
Then Sorrowe cease, and wipe thy weeping eye;
For Fame shall live, when all the World shall dye.   270

Finis.

The Combat, betweene Conscience and Covetousness, in the minde of Man.

—quid non mortalia pectora cogis
Auri sacra fames? Virgil

London,
Printed by G.S. for John Jaggard,
and are to be solde at his shoppe
neere Temple-barre,
at the Signe of the Hand and starre.
1598.

To his Worshipfull good friend,
Maister *John Steventon, of Dothill,*
in the County of *Salop,* Esquire.

Sith Conscience (long since) is exilde the Citty,
O let her in the Countrey, finde some Pitty:
But if she be exilde, the Countrey too,
O let her finde, some favour yet of you.

The Combat, betweene Conscience and Covetousnesse, in the mind of Man.

Now had the cole-blacke steedes, of pitchie Night,
(Breathing out Darknesse) banisht cheerfull Light,
And sleepe (the shaddowe of eternall rest)
My severall senses, wholy had possest.
When loe, there was presented to my view,
A vision strange, yet not so strange, as true.
Conscience (me thought) appeared unto mee,
Cloth'd with good Deedes, with Trueth and Honestie,
Her countinance demure, and sober sad,
Nor any other Ornament shee had.   10
Then *Covetousnesse* did incounter her,
Clad in a Cassock, lyke a Usurer,
The Cassock, it was made of poore-mens skinnes,
Lac'd here and there, with many severall sinnes:
Nor was it furd, with any common furre;
Or if it were, himselfe hee was the *fur.*

A Bag of money, in his hande he helde,
The which with hungry eie, he still behelde.
The place wherein this vision first began,
(A spacious plaine) was cald *The Minde of Man.*   20
The Carle no sooner, *Conscience* had espyde,
But swelling lyke a Toade, (puft up with pryde)
He straight began against her to invey:
These were the wordes, which *Covetise* did sey.
Conscience (quoth hee) how dar'st thou bee so bold,
To claime the place, that I by right doe hold?
Neither by right, nor might, thou canst obtain it:
By might (thou knowst full well) thou canst not gaine it.
The greatest Princes are my followars,
The King in Peace, the Captaine in the Warres: 30
The Courtier, and the simple Countrey-man:
The Judge, the Merchant, and the Gentleman:
The learned Lawyer, and the Politician:
The skilfull Surgeon, and the fine Physician:
In briefe, all sortes of men mee entertaine,
And hold mee, as their Soules sole Soveraigne,
And in my quarrell, they will fight and die,
Rather then I should suffer injurie.
And as for title, interest, and right,
Ile prove its mine by that, as well as might,   40
Though *Covetousnesse,* were used long before,
Yet Judas Treason, made my Fame the more;
When *Christ* he caused, crucifyde to bee,
For thirtie pence, man solde his minde to mee:
And now adaies, what tenure is more free,
Than that which purchas'd is, with gold and fee?

Conscience.
With patience, have I heard thy large Complaint,

Wherein the Divell, would be thought a Saint:
But wot ye what, the Saying is of olde?
One tale is good, untill anothers tolde. 50
Truth is the right, that I must stand upon,
(For other title, hath poore *Conscience* none)
First I will prove it, by Antiquitie,
That thou are but an up-start, unto mee;
Before that thou wast ever thought upon,
The minde of Man, belonged to mee alone.
For after that the Lord, hath Man created,
And him in blisse-full Paradice had seated;
(Knowing his Nature was to vice inclynde)
God gave me unto man, to rule his mynde, 60
And as it were, his Governour to bee,
To guide his minde, in Trueth, and Honestie.
And where thou sayst, that man did sell his soule;
That Argument, I quicklie can controule:
It is a fayned fable, thou doost tell,
That, which is not his owne, he cannot sell;
No man can sell his soule, altho he thought it:
Mans soule is Christs, for hee hath dearely bought it.
Therefore usurping *Covetise*, be gone.
For why, the minde belongs to mee alone. 70

Covetousnesse.
Alas poor *Conscience*, how thou art deceav'd?
As though of sense, thou wert quite bereavd.
What wilt thou say (that thinkst thou canst not erre)
If I can prove my selfe the ancienter?
Though into Adams minde, God did infuse thee,
Before his fall, yet man did never use thee.
What was it else, but *Avarice* in *Eve*,
(Thinking thereby, in greater Blisse to live)

That made her taste, of the forbidden fruite?
Of her Desier, was not I the roote?   80
Did she not covet? (tempted by the Devill)
The Apple of the Tree, of good and evill?
Before man used *Conscience,* she did covet:
Therefore by her Transgression, here I prove it,
That *Covetousnesse* possest the minde of man,
Before that any *Conscience* began.

Conscience.
Even as a counterfeited precious stone,
Seemes to bee far more rich, to looke upon,
Then doeth the right: But when a man comes neere,
His baseness then, doeth evident appeere: 90
So *Covetise,* the Reasons thou dooest tell,
Seeme to be strong, but being weighed well,
They are indeed, but onely meere Illusions,
And doe inforce but very weake Conclusions.
When as the Lord (fore-knowing his offence)
Had given man a Charge, of Abstinence,
And to refraine, the fruite of good and ill:
Man had a *Conscience,* to obey his will,
And never would be tempted thereunto,
Untill the Woeman, shee, did worke *man woe.*   100
And make him breake, the Lords Commaundement,
Which all Mankinde, did afterward repent:
So that thou seest, thy Argument is vaine,
And I am prov'd, the elder of the twaine.

Covetousnesse.
Fond Wretch, it was not *Conscience,* but feare,
That made the first man (Adam) to forbeare
To tast the fruite, of the forbidden Tree,

Lest, if offending hee were found to bee,
(According as Jehovah saide on hye,
For his so great Transgression, hee should dye.)   110
Feare curbd his minde, it was not *Conscience* then,
(For *Conscience* freely, rules the harts of men)
And is a godly motion of the mynde,
To everie vertuous action inclynde,
And not enforc'd through feare of Punishment,
But is to vertue, voluntary bent:
Then (simple Trul) be packing pressentlie,
For in this place, there is no roome for thee.

Conscience.
Aye mee, (distressed Wight) what shall I doe?
Where shall I rest? Or whither shall I goe?   120
Unto the rich? (Woes mee) They, doe abhor me:
Unto the poore? (Alas) they, care not for me:
Unto the Olde-man? hee, hath mee forgot:
Unto the Young-man? Yet hee, knowes me not.
Unto the Prince? Hee, can dispence with me:
Unto the Magristrate? that, may not bee:
Unto the Court? For it, I am too base:
Unto the country? There, I have no place:
Unto the Citty? Thence, I am exilde:
Unto the Village? there, I am revilde: 130
Unto the Barre? the Lawyer there, is bribed:
Unto the Warre? there, *Conscience* is derided:
Unto the Temple? there, I am disguised:
Unto the Market? there, I am despised
Thus both the young and olde, the rich and poore,
Against mee (silly Creature) shut their doore.
Then, sith each one seekes my rebuke and shame,
Ile goe againe to Heaven (from whence I came.)

This saide (me thought) making exceeding mone,
She went her way, and left the Carle alone,   140
Who vaunting of his late-got victorie,
Advanc'd himselfe in pompe and Majestie:
Much like a Cocke, who having kild his foe,
Brisks up himselfe, and then begins to crow.
So *Covetise*, when *Conscience* was departed,
Gan to be proud in minde, and hauty harted:
And in a stately Chayre of state he set him,
(For *Conscience* banisht) there was none to let him.
And being but one entrie, to this Plaine,
(Whereof as king and Lord, he did remaine)   150
Repentance cald, he causd that to be kept,
Lest *Conscience* should returne, whilst as he slept:
Wherefore he causd it, to be watcht and warded
Both night and Day, and to be strongly guarded:
To keepe it safe, these three he did intreat,
Hardnesse of hart, with *Falshood* and *Deceat*:
And if at any time, she chaunc'd to venter,
Hardnesse of hart, denide her still to enter.
When *Conscience* was exilde the minde of Man,
Then *Covetise*, his government began.   160
This once being seene, what I had seene before,
(Being onely seene in sleepe) was seene no more:
For with the sorrowe, which my Soule did take
At sight hereof, foorthwith I did awake.

Finis

Poems
In divers humors.

Trahit sua quemque voluptas. Virgil.

London,
Printed by G.S. for John Jaggard,
and are to be solde at his shoppe
neere Temple-barre,
at the Signe of the Hand and starre.
1598.

To the learned, and accomplisht Gentleman,
Maister *Nicholas Blackleech*, of Grayes Inne.

To you, that know the tuch of true Conceat;
(Whose many gifts I neede not to repeat)
I write these Lines; fruits of unriper yeares;
Wherein my Muse no harder censure feares:
Hoping in gentle Worth, you will them take;
Not for the gift, but for the givers sake.

SONNET I

To his friend Maister R.L.
In praise of Musique and Poetrie

If Musique and sweet Poetrie agree,
As they must needes (the Sister and the Brother)
Then must the Love be great, twixt thee and mee,
Because thou lov'st the one, and I the other.
Dowland to thee is deare; whose heavenly tuch
Upon the Lute, doeth ravish humaine sense:
Spenser to mee; whose deepe Conceit is such,
As passing all Conceit, needs no defence.
Thou lov'st to heare the sweete melodious sound,
That *Phoebus* Lute (the Queene of Musique) makes:
And I in deepe Delight am chiefly drownd,
When as himselfe to singing he betakes.
One God is God of Both (as Poets faigne)
One Knight loves Both, and Both in thee remaine.

SONNET II

Against the Dispraysers of Poetrie.

Chaucer is dead; and *Gower* lyes in grave;
The Earle of *Surrey,* long agoe is gone,
Sir *Philip Sidneis* soule, the Heavens have;
George Gascoigne him beforne, was tomb'd in stone,
Yet, tho their Bodies lye full low in ground,
(As every thing must dye, that earst was borne)
Their living fame, no Fortune can confound;
Nor ever shall their Labours be forlorne.
And you, that discommend sweete Poetrie,
(So that the Subject of the same be good)
Here may you see, your fond simplicitie;
Sith Kings have favord it, of royall Blood.
The King of *Scots* (now living) is a Poet,
As his *Lepanto,* and his *Furies* shoe it.

A Remembrance of some English Poets.

Live *Spenser* ever, in thy *Fairy Queene:*
Whose like (for deepe Conceit) was never seene:
Crownd mayst thou bee, unto thy more renowne,
(As King of Poets) with a Lawrell Crowne.

And *Daniell,* praised for thy sweet-chast Verse:
Whose Fame is grav'd on *Rosamonds* blacke Herse.
Still mayst thou live: and still be honored,
For that rare Worke, *The White Rose and the Red.*

And *Drayton,* whose wel-written Tragedies,
And sweete Epistles, soare thy fame to skies,

Thy learned Name, is aequall with the rest;
Whose stately Numbers are so well addrest.

And *Shakespeare* thou, whose hony-flowing Vaine,
(Pleasing the World) thy Praises doth obtaine.
Whose *Venus*, and whose *Lucrece* (sweete, and chaste)
Thy Name in fames immortall Booke have plac't.
Live ever you, at least in Fame live ever:
Well may the Bodye dye, but Fame dies never.

An Ode

As it fell upon a Day
In the merrie Month of May,
Sitting in a pleasant shade,
Which a grove of Myrtles made,
Beastes did leape, and Birds did sing,
Trees did grow, and Plants did spring:
Everything did banish mone,
Save the Nightingale alone.
Shee (poore Bird) as all forlorne,
Leand her Breast up-till a thorne;   10
And there sung the dolefulst Ditty,
That to heare it was great Pitty.
Fie, fie, fie, now would she cry
Teru Teru, by and by:
That to heare her so complaine,
Scarce I could from Teares refraine:
For her griefes so lively showne,
Made me thinke upon mine owne.
Ah (thought I) thou mournst in vaine;
None takes Pitty on thy paine: 20
Senslesse Trees, they cannot heere thee;

Ruthlesse Beares, they wil not cheer thee.
King *Pandion,* hee is dead:
All thy friends are lapt in Lead.
All thy fellow Birds doe singe,
Carelesse of thy sorrowing.
Whilst as fickle Fortune smilde,
Thou and I, were both beguilde.
Everie one that flatters thee,
Is no friend in miserie: 30
Words are easie, like the winde;
Faithfull friends are hard to finde:
Everie man will bee thy friend,
Whilst thou hast wherewith to spend:
But if store of Crownes be scant,
No man will supply thy want.
If that one be prodigall,
Bountifull, they will him call:
And with such-like flattering,
Pitty but hee were a King.   40
If hee bee adict to vice,
Quickly him, they will intice.
If to Woemen hee be bent,
They have at Commaundement.
But if Fortune once doe frowne,
Then farewell his great renowne:
They that fawnd on him before,
Use his company no more.
Hee that is thy friend indeed,
Hee will helpe thee in thy neede: 50
If thou sorrowe, hee will weepe;
If thou wake, hee cannot sleepe:
Thus of everie griefe, in hart
Hee, with thee, doeth beare a Part.

These are certaine signes, to knowe
Faithfull friend, from flatt'ring foe.

Written, at the Request of a Gentleman, under a Gentlewomans Picture.

Even as *Apelles* could not paint *Campaspes* face aright,
Because *Campaspes* sun-bright eyes did dimme *Apelles* sight:
Even so, amazed at her sight, her sight, all sights excelling,
Like *Nyobe* the Painter stoode, her sight his sight expelling,
Thus Art and Nature did contend, who should the Victor bee,
Till Art by Nature was supprest, as all the worlde may see.

An Epitaph upon the Death, of Sir Philip Sidney, Knight: Lord-Governour of Vlissing.

That *England* lost, that Learning lov'd, that every mouth
   commended,
That fame did prayse, that Prince did rayse, that Countrey so
   defended,
Here lyes the man: lyke to the Swan, who knowing she shall die,
Doeth tune her voice unto the Spheares, and scornes Mortalitie.
Two worthie Earles his uncles were; a Lady was his Mother;
A Knight his father; and himselfe a noble Countesse Brother.
Belov'd, bewaild; alive, now dead; of all, with Teares for ever;
Here lyes Sir *Philip Sidneis* Corps, whom cruell Death did sever.
He liv'd for her, hee dyde for her; for whom he dyde, he lived:
O graunt (O God) that wee of her, may never be deprived.

An Epitaph upon the Death of his Aunt, Mistresse Elizabeth Skrymsher.

Loe here beholde the certaine Ende, of every living wight:
No Creature is secure from death, for Death will have his Right.

He spareth none: both rich and poore, both young and olde must
   die;
So fraile is flesh, so short is Life, so sure Mortalitie.
When first the Bodye lives to Life, the soule first dies to sinne:
And they that loose this early Life, a heavenly Life shall winne,
If they live well: as well she liv'd, that lyeth Under heere;
Whose Vertuous Life to all the Worlde, most plainly did appeere.
Good to the poore, friend to the rich, and foe to no Degree:
A President of modest Life, and peerelesse Chastitie.
Who loving more, Who more belov'd, of everie honest mynde?
Who more to Hospitalitie, and Clemencie inclinde
Then she? that being buried here, lyes wrapt in Earth below;
From whence we came, to whom wee must, and be as shee is now,
A Clodd of Clay: though her pure soule in endlesse Blisse doeth
   rest;
Joying all joy, the Place of Peace, prepared for the blest:
Where holy Angells sit and sing, before the King of Kings;
Not mynding worldly Vanities, but onely heavenly Things.
Unto which joy, Unto which Blisse, Unto which Place of Pleasure,
God graunt that wee may come at least, t'injoy that heavenly
   Treasure.
Which to obtaine, to live as shee hath done let us endevor;
That wee may live with Christ himselfe, (above) that lives for ever.

A Comparison of the Life of Man.

Mans life is well compared to a feast,
Furnisht with choice of all Varietie:
To it comes Tyme; and as a bidden guest
Hee sets him downe in Pompe and Majestie;
The three-folde Age of Man, the Waiters bee:

Then with an earthen voyder (made of clay)
Comes Death, and takes the table clean away.

Finis.

Dubia

My prime of youth is but a froste of cares.
My feaste of Joy is but a dish of paine.
My cropp of corne is but a feild of tares.
and all my good is but vayne hope of gayne
The day is paste and yet I saw no sonne
And now I live and now my life is donne
My tale was harde, and yet it was not told
my frute is faine, and yet my leaves are greene
My youth is spent and yet I am not old.
I saw ye world and yet I was not seene
My thread is cut, and yet it is not sponne
And now I live and now my lief is donne.
I sought my death and found it in my wombe.
I lookt for life and saw it was a shade.
I trod ye yearth and knewe it was my tombe
And now I die, and now I was but made
My glasse is full and now my glasse is runne
And now I live and now my lief is donne.

Answer.

Thy prime of youth is frozen wth thy faultes
Thy feaste of Joy is finisht wth thy fall.
Thy cropp of corne is tares a vayling naughtes
Thy good god knowes thy hope, thy happ and all.

Short were thy daies and shadow was thy sonne

T'obscure thy light unluckely begunne.

Time trieth truth and truth, hath treason tript

Thy faith bare fruite, as thou hadste faithlesse beene.

Thine ill spent youth, thyne after yeares have impte.

and god y^t sawe thee, hath prservd our Queene

Her thride still holdes thine perisht thowth unspune.

And she shall live when trayters lives are donne.

Thou soughtst thy death, and found it in deserte

Thou lookst for lief yet lewdIy forcd it fade

Thou trodst the earth and now in earth thou arte

As men may wish yu nevr hadst bin made

Thy glory and thy glasse are tymeles runne

And this (O Tuchbourne) hath thy Treason donne.

Finis.

Wife

The double U, is dowble woe

The I, is nought but jelosie

The F, is fawninge flatterie

The E is nought but enmitie.

Thus U wth I, wth f, wth E:

Brings nothinge els but miserie.

Answere.

Is double U such double woe

Speake of no more then that you knowe.

Tis weale, tis wealth, and nothing soe.

I, Joye is, not jealosie.

F favor is, not flattery.

E is true loves eternytie.

Thus, U, wth I, wth F, wth E
well consterd is felicitie.

Finis

To the right Worthy Sir John Spenser Knighte Alderman of the Honnorable Citty of London and lorde treasurer of Lady pecunia.

Led by the swifte reporte of winged fame,
with golden trumpet soundinge forth your name,
To you I dedicate this merry Muse
And for my Patron I your favor chuse,
She is a woman shee muste be respected
Shee is a Queene she muste not be rejected
This is the shaddowe you the substance have
Which substance nowe this shaddowe seemes to crave.

Richard Barnfild.

Finis.

There is a thinge y^t much is usd
tis caulled love, by men abusd:
they write and sigh and sweare they die
when all is done they know they lie,
but when they sweare by faith & troth
ile sweare they care not for an othe.

They firste muste have a mistres faire
and then a favor for to weare
and then they go to flattries skoole
and call her wise they knowe a foole

but let them sweare by faith and troth
ile sweare they care not for an othe.

It is a practise in this age
to lay theire creditts unto gage,
by wit by vowes by neate attire
to conquer that they most desire
but let them sweare by faith and troth
ile sweare they care not for an othe.

Finis.

A lustie nutt browne wenche scant woorth ye naminge
went downe a steaier bearinge a candle flaming:
A swagering gallant comming her t'encounter
att first approache couragiously would mount her:
Shee strongly made resistaunce and did sware
she would burne him by that candie she did beare:
Hee blew ye candle out to breake hir vowe
she kept her promise still, immagine how.

Finis.

Sweete hart to deale trewly I love thee not much
disdaininge to serve thee thy kindnes is such;
For why thy demeanor commendeth thee not
thy bewty unpleasing the better my lott:
Then sweete I assure you ile love you not more,
refusinge to love you which loved you before.

Finis.

The Unknowne Sheepheards Complaint

My Flocks feede not, my Ewes breede not,
My Rammes speede not, all is amisse:
Love is denying, Faith is defying,
Harts renying, causer of this.
All my merry Jiggs are quite forgot,
All my Ladies love is lost God wot.
Where her faith was firmely fixt in love.
There a nay is plac'd without remove.
One silly crosse, wrought all my losse,
O frowning Fortune, cursed fickle Dame:
For now I see, inconstancie
More in women then in men remaine.

In black mourne I, all feares scorne I,
Love hath forlorne me, living in thrall:
Hart is bleeding, all helpe needing,
O cruell speeding, fraughted with gall.
My Sheepheards pipe can sound no deale,
My Weathers bell rings dolefull knell.
My curtaile dogge that wont to have plaide,
Playes not at all, but seemes afraide.
With sighs so deepe, procures to weepe,
In howling-wise, to see my dolefull plight:
How sighs resound, through hartlesse ground,
Like a thousand vanquish'd men in bloody fight.

Cleare Wells spring not, sweet birds sing not,
Greene plants bring not foorth their die:
Heards stand weeping, Flocks all sleeping,
Nimphs back peeping fearefully.
All our pleasure knowne to us poore Swaines,
All our merry meeting on the Plaines.

All our evening sports from us are fled,
All our love is lost, for Love is dead.
Farewell sweete Love, thy like nere was,
For sweete content, the cause of all my moane:
Poore *Coridon* must live alone,
Other helpe for him, I see that there is none.

Selected Bibliography

Barnfield, Richard. *The Complete Poems*. Ed. Alexander B. Grosart. London, 1876.

_____. *Poems*. Ed. Edward Arber. Birmingham, 1882.

_____. *Poems*. Ed. Montague Summers. London, 1936.

_____. *The Complete Poems*. Ed. George Klawitter. Selinsgrove: Susquehanna University Press, 1990.

Borris, Kenneth and George Klawitter, eds. *The Affectionate Shepherd: Celebrating Richard Barnfield*. Selinsgrove: Susquehanna University Press, 2001.

Borris, Kenneth. "'Ile hang a bag and a bottle at thy back.'" In Borris, *The Affectionate Shepherd*. 193-248.

_____. R[ichard] B[arnfield]'s Homosocial Engineering in *Orpheus His Journey to Hell*." In Borris, *The Affectionate Shepherd*. 332-360.

Charles, Casey. "Barnfield's Lover's Discourse." In Borris, *The Affectionate Shepherd*. 174-192.

Daugherty, Leo. "The Question of Topical Allusion in Richard Barnfield's Pastoral Verse." In Borris, *The Affectionate Shepherd*. 45-61.

DeNeef, A. Leigh. "The Poetics of Orpheus: The Text and a Study of *Orpheus His Journey to Hell* (1595)." *Studies in Philology* (1992): 20-70.

DiGangi, Mario. "'My Plentie Makes Me Poore': Linguistic and Erotic Failure in 'The Affectionate Shepheard.'" In Borris, *The Affectionate Shepherd*. 149-173.

Ellis, Jim. "Orpheus at the Inns of Court." In Borris, *The Affectionate Shepherd*. 283-304.

Folkerth, Wes. "The Metamorphosis of Daphnis: The Case for Richard Barnfield's *Orpheus*." In Borris, *The Affectionate Shepherd*. 305-331.

Frontain, Raymond-Jean. "'An Affectionate Shepheard sicke for Love': Barnfield's Homoerotic Appropriation of the Song of Solomon." In Borris, *The Affectionate Shepherd*. 99-114.

Giantvalley, Scott. "Barnfield, Drayton, and Marlowe: Homoeroticism and Homosexuality in Elizabethan Literature." *Pacific Coast Philology* 16 (1981): 9-24.

Malpezzi, Frances. "Barnfield's Variations on the Theme of Avarice in *Lady Pecunia*." In Borris, *The Affectionate Shepherd*. 151-262.

Morris, Harry. *Richard Barnfield, Colin's Child*. Tampa: Florida State University Studies, 1963.

Norton, Rictor. "Pastoral Homoeroticism and Barnfield, the Affectionate Shepherd." In Borris, *The Affectionate Shepherd*. 117-129.

Prescott, Anne Lake. "Barnfield's Spenser: 'Great Collin' and the Art of Denial." In Borris, *The Affectionate Shepherd*. 85-98.

Theodore, David. "'Gay is the right word': Montague Summers and the Replevin of Richard Barnfield." In Borris, *The Affectionate Shepherd*. 265-279.

Worrall, Andrew. "Barnfield's Feast of 'all Varietie.'" In Borris, *The Affectionate Shepherd*. 25-40.

Yen, Julie W. "'If it be sinne to love a sweet-fac'd Boy': Rereading Homoerotic Desire in Barnfield's Ganymede Poems." In Borris, *The Affectionate Shepherd*. 130-148.

978-0-595-36798-6
0-595-36798-4

3387542